# WILL ROGERS STORYTELLER

## American Humor from the Beginnings to the Oklahoma Cowboy

Dennis M. Clausen

Mechanicsburg, PA USA

Published by Sunbury Press, Inc.
Mechanicsburg, PA USA

**www.sunburypress.com**



For information about special discounts for bulk purchases, please contact Sunbury Press Orders Dept. at (855) 338-8359 or orders@sunburypress.com.

To request one of our authors for speaking engagements or book signings, please contact Sunbury Press Publicity Dept. at publicity@sunburypress.com.

FIRST SUNBURY PRESS EDITION: March 2026

Set in Adobe Garamond | Interior design by Crystal Devine | Cover by Lawrence Knorr | Edited by Abigail Bunner.

Publisher's Cataloging-in-Publication Data
Names: Clausen, Dennis M., author.
Title: Will Rogers storyteller : American humor from the beginnings to the Oklahoma cowboy / Dennis M. Clausen.
Description: First trade paperback edition. | Mechanicsburg, PA : Sunbury Press, 2026.
Summary: Will Rogers is one of the most unifying figures in American and World history. His ever-widening magical lasso encircled the globe and encouraged people everywhere to ignore their differences and live as one. We need his voice as much today as when he was captivating audiences with his boyish charm and homespun wisdom. His gift of laughter was a gift of hope.
Identifiers: ISBN : 979-8-88819-425-6 (softcover).
Subjects: HISTORY / United States / 19th Century | HISTORY / United States / State & Local / Middle Atlantic (DC, DE, MD, NJ, NY, PA) | BIOGRAPHY & AUTOBIOGRAPHY / Historical.

Designed in the USA
0 1 1 2 3 5 8 13 21 34 55

*For the Love of Books!*

# Contents

# ACKNOWLEDGMENTS

MY WIFE, Alexa, has been a partner in every sense in providing historical research and reading the early drafts of this book. As a retired historian for the California State Park system, she helped create the original "General Plan" for the Will Rogers State Historic Park. Her knowledge of that history, and the intricacies of historical resources and sites in general, have been invaluable in the writing of this book.

Lawrence Knorr, publisher, and others at Sunbury Press have provided ongoing support for all of my books that have been published by their subsidiary, Brown Posey Press. Publishing Assistant Nicole Brown and Assistant Editor Abigail Bunner provided support and editorial advice at various stages of this project. Katie Cressman, digital marketing, has also provided valuable assistance in several areas of preparing this book for publication. Crystal Devine, book designer for Sunbury Press, organized and shaped the text and photos in the final stages of the development of Will Rogers Storyteller.

Liza A. Donath retyped the entire manuscript so it was compatible with Microsoft Word. The original manuscript was in WordStar—yes, I'm sure many people haven't heard that word in a long time—which proved to be resistant to conversion to Microsoft Word. Fortunately, I had saved some print copies of the original manuscripts, and Liza was able to create a workable draft for me to edit and expand into its current form.

Rebecca Crowther, photo archivist at the California State Parks Statewide Museum Collections Center, searched state parks photo archives and provided thumbnail sketches to select final photos for this book.

Susan Lamb, principal lLibrarian at the Santa Monica Public Library, provided scans of photos from the Pacific Palisades Historical Society Image Collection at the Santa Monica Library.

The University of San Diego and my colleagues in the English Department have provided support for this and my previous works of fiction and nonfiction. That support has always been appreciated.

Ashley Hayes, archivist for the City of Escondido's Pioneer Room, graciously allowed my wife and me to use her facilities for a variety of reasons as we prepared the various drafts of this book. She was especially helpful in enabling me to view and work with some of the photographs that were eventually incorporated into the text.

Jon May, photo archivist for the Oklahoma Historical Society, provided assistance with granting permissions and links to downloads from their collections.

To all the earlier researchers and historians who kept the American past accessible to future generations, and whose works were unfortunately consumed by the wildfires that destroyed much of the Will Rogers State Historic Park, I am deeply indebted. Those books were instrumental in helping me research and write the first drafts of this book in the early 1990s. Fortunately, other libraries still have those books so their many insights can be shared by future generations and scholars. I hope I have done justice to their earlier efforts to keep our nation's history alive so we can all move more wisely into the future.

Although various people and sources in the California State Park system are the last to be acknowledged, they are certainly not the least in importance. These park employees, together with my wife, provided support throughout the research and various drafts of this book. California State Park employees also did everything in their power, even putting their own lives at risk, to save whatever they could from the Will Rogers ranch before it burned to the ground. Those efforts saved at least some of the priceless resources Will Rogers and his wife Betty donated to the state of California. Hopefully, what they managed to protect will someday provide the foundations to rebuild the Will Rogers State Historic Park so future generations will be able to visit and learn the lessons the Oklahoma cowboy bequeathed to a grateful nation.

# A PERSONAL NOTE FROM THE AUTHOR

On January 8, 2025, I awoke and immediately turned on the television set. Like everyone else in Southern California, I wondered how the efforts to control the wildfires that were roaring out of the Santa Monica Mountains were faring. I quickly learned that Pacific Palisades, a mountainous region eighteen miles west of Los Angeles, was on fire everywhere. Later that day, I learned the historic structures and artifacts in the Will Rogers State Park in Pacific Palisades were almost completely destroyed. A ranger station was the only building that had survived. The rest of the state park had been reduced to charred ruins of what had once been Will Rogers's ranch home and other structures that contained the mementos of his legacy.

The wildfires reminded me that I had a special connection to the Will Rogers State Park. In the early 1990s my wife worked as a historian for the California State Parks. One of her assignments was to help develop a "General Plan" for the park. Her specific assignment included the area of Pacific Palisades where Will Rogers's ranch home, barns, and museum were located.

On one of her trips to the park, she invited me to go with her. I had done some research on Will Rogers during my graduate programs in American studies at the University of Minnesota and again at the University of California, Riverside. The opportunity to visit the home where he actually lived for much of his adult life was appealing.

It was to be the first of many trips we made to his ranch home. Each time, while my wife concentrated on her research, I sat for hours in the library where Will Rogers's personal books were stored. Other books, often in the western genre, were added to the library after he died. I was told that all of the furniture and artworks were the same as when the Rogers family lived there. As I paged through the books and sat in the chairs where he sat, I started to feel a personal connection to the legendary man the world came to know as the "Oklahoma cowboy."

When I wasn't in his library, I roamed through the other rooms in his house and out into the surrounding field where he played polo with his friends. It wasn't hard to visualize him on horseback, grinning broadly and enjoying the friendships of people with whom he felt most comfortable. I knew of his Cherokee background, and I wondered if perhaps riding his horse around the polo field would put him in touch with some deeper source of his ancestry.

Those trips to Will Rogers's California home put me in touch with the man I had first seen in films in the Minnesota small-town theaters of my youth. I could feel his presence in the rooms in his ranch house, and I wanted to know more about him. As I sat in one of his chairs, I decided to start writing a book on his earlier years growing up in Oklahoma. Many of my sources were the books I found in his personal library. From those books and interviews with Rogers I had read, I realized he was deeply familiar with the history of the American westward movement and how it had affected his own Cherokee ancestry.

Later that summer, Alexa and I took a trip to Minnesota. We decided to take a long detour to visit the Will Rogers Memorial Museum in Claremore, Oklahoma. My memories of that museum are somewhat less clear than my memories of the ranch and museum in Pacific Palisades. However, I did gain a much clearer sense of Will Rogers, the goodwill ambassador, humanitarian, and American celebrity who gained both national and international fame before his tragic death in a plane crash in 1935.

At the Claremore museum, we asked one of the attendants if the Will Rogers home was anywhere nearby and if tourists were allowed to visit it. She graciously put us in touch with an elderly man who, "since we had driven all the way from California," offered to escort us out to the restored Rogers family home.

The ranch house, we were told, had been moved to a more accessible area, but tourists could only enter it during certain times of the year.

Our elderly tour guide told us we could at least see what it looked like during Will Rogers's early formative years. Our guide drove ahead of us in a pickup truck, and we followed closely behind. I was intrigued by the Oklahoma prairie landscape because it looked very much like the Minnesota prairie near the South Dakota border where I had grown up.

I had lived the early years of my life on a farm in West Central Minnesota fifteen miles from the nearest town. Later in my life, I lived for a time with my uncle and aunt in another very rural, isolated part of Minnesota. My ancestral background includes a great-grandfather and his wife who were among the first settlers in that area. They built a sod house and lived in it for a couple of years before they could build a frame house. Rural poverty was also something I had experienced in my youth, as were the open, rolling Midwestern prairie lands that seemingly extended into the horizon in all directions. The lonely, yet somehow beautiful emptiness of that world still lingered in my memories.

As we approached the house, I was surprised by its appearance. It was clear from the roomy, two-story home that Will Rogers did not come from an impoverished background. Nor did he come from a wealthy background, at least as measured by East Coast or West Coast standards. He was part of the great middle- and upper-middle classes that clung to the traditional dreams of the earlier settlers who had forged across the continent and often settled in the Midwest.

Perhaps I was reading too much into Will Rogers's background, but it seemed to me he was not really a part of any strictly defined social class. He was more a product of his Cherokee, white American combined heritage that the nation itself had to address before it could even become a nation.

We spent some time looking at Will Rogers's home from a distance. As I stared at the house, I kept wondering how Will Rogers could have grown up in such a luxurious home in the middle of the Midwestern prairie. It just didn't match the preconceptions of where I had imagined he might have lived in his youth.

When we returned to California after our trip to the Midwest, I was even more determined to write a book about the Oklahoma cowboy and national icon who captured the imagination of the American people in so many ways. His life seemed to be a series of contradictions between competing forces. Yet, he seemed to have combined those competing forces into a positive, even uplifting view of America in spite of its cruelty to his Native American ancestors.

I decided early that I wanted the book to be more than an academic study, although there are certainly elements of that in the text. The book, as it evolved, became a personal journey to understand a man who had intrigued me since I was a boy watching him perform seemingly impossible rope tricks on the movie screens in the small-town theaters of my youth.

I worked on the book for several years in between my academic and other responsibilities. Then I had to put the project aside as other writing and publishing contracts took priority. The manuscript and supplemental materials slowly descended into the lower echelons of my office bookcase, filled with other projects I had put on hold over the years.

It probably would have remained on those dust-covered, out-of-sight bookshelves if it hadn't been for another coincidence. A few weeks after the wildfires destroyed Will Rogers's ranch home in Pacific Palisades, I embarked on a mundane project all writers must occasionally address. I had run out of room in my home office and was trying to remove the clutter when I spotted the folder that contained the drafts of the book on Will Rogers I planned someday to complete and publish. I removed the clutter from a chair and sat down to read a few pages of the manuscript. Almost immediately, I was again captivated by the man who had intrigued me so profoundly while I sat in his ranch home library over thirty years earlier and read through some of his books. Sadly, those books, like almost everything else in Will Rogers State Park, were destroyed in the wildfires.

Somewhere in the haze of all those memories I realized that in another ten years, on August 15, 2035, we would be honoring Will Rogers 100 years after he died in Point Barrow, Alaska. I also realized on July 4, 2026, we would be celebrating the 250th anniversary of the founding of our country. Those two dates resonated in ways I had not expected. I became convinced we would soon be embarking on a journey to rediscover and reexamine the people who had made America possible.

One of those people was Will Rogers. I had some questions that had been dormant in my mind for many years. Now, it was time to ask those questions again. Why did Will Rogers's humor resonate so deeply with the American people? Were there others like him, or was he one of a kind? What forces created the man who became a celebrity and then an almost epic folk hero to many Americans?

With the images of the smoldering ruins of Pacific Palisades on our television screen still fresh in my mind, I decided to take another shot at completing the book about Will Rogers, a man who was still a mystery to me—but also a man who might be more important to America today than ever before in our history.

His gift of laughter was a gift of hope.

*NOTE: With the exception of "150 priceless artifacts," including Will's typewriter that park employees managed to throw into their vehicles before fleeing from the wildfires on January 7, 2025, the contents of Will Rogers's library were destroyed. The many references in this book,* Will Rogers Storyteller, *are mostly to the books and written materials I read and reviewed over thirty years earlier when I sat in his library and home. I kept those footnotes and bibliography in their original form as though the books and the library still existed. Perhaps it is a concession to nostalgia. Or perhaps it is a testimonial to the books he actually used to help create the legacy of the Oklahoma cowboy.*

# PREFACE

WHEN WILL Rogers died in the tragic airplane crash in Point Barrow, Alaska, on August 15, 1935, every American knew we had lost someone special. The outpouring of national grief was overwhelming. No other public figure in the twentieth century had touched the hearts of the American people as deeply as Will Rogers and his Oklahoma cowboy. As radio stations and newspapers broadcast the news of Will Rogers's death, many Americans felt as though something irreplaceable had been torn out of the nation's soul, leaving behind the emptiest of voids.

Today, as we leave the twentieth century behind us, there are many symbols and images that we immediately associate with this most turbulent period in American history: an old beat-up pick-up truck packed high with a family's entire belongings as it moved slowly through a dust storm while searching for a new home during the Great Depression; military vessels twisted into blackened, smoldering heaps of metal in Pearl Harbor; radioactive mushroom clouds billowing ominously over the New Mexico deserts; President John F. Kennedy's black limousine moving slowly, tragically through Dealey Plaza; helicopters swirling in packs over Southeast Asian jungles and tropical forests. These and a host of other historical images remind us, as they will remind future historians, of the twentieth century and the apocalyptic forces it unleashed that seemed constantly to threaten the nation's and even the world's survival.

But nothing in the twentieth century is so typically American as the gum-chewing, lasso-twirling Oklahoma cowboy Will Rogers created for his vaudeville act and later refined for the electronic media. When Will Rogers created this stage and literary character, he reached deeper into the wellsprings of American cultural values than any performer before or after his death. Through the Oklahoma cowboy, Will Rogers created the very archetypal symbol of American cultural values. We loved, and continue to love this character precisely because he reminds us of the best things we see in ourselves and our nation.

Many of the other images we associate with twentieth-century America have been neatly consigned to the pages of history. The Oklahoma cowboy, however, continues to perform rope tricks and tell jokes as he walks the invisible stages in the collective memories of the American people long after his creator perished in Point Barrow, Alaska. He continues to live inside each and every one of us because he is the inevitable culmination of the various cultural forces that shaped this nation and its values from the time, many centuries earlier, when the first European settlers arrived in the New World. The lasso he used on stage, and once to drag a rampaging bull out of the audience during a rodeo performance, would eventually encircle the entire nation and even the world with its magic.

Will Rogers is a product of the late nineteenth and early twentieth centuries, but he ultimately transcends that period of time in American history. He is with us precisely because he has always been with us and will always be with us. Will Rogers's creative genius took the more positive aspects of the American experience in the New World, especially our evolving sense of humor, and he created the Oklahoma cowboy who will outlive all of us—and maybe even the nation itself.

Dennis M. Clausen

# I.

# OKLAHOMA COWBOY: "PERSON" OR "PERSONA"[1]

WILL ROGERS (1879–1935), America's most beloved twentieth-century humorist, is considered by many of his admirers to be an "original." He was part Cherokee, part authentic Oklahoma cowboy, who came into this world with a gift that enabled him to develop his own unique, folksy brand of humor. Those who view Will Rogers in this context are quick to point out that his early life experiences among the dying breed of western cowboys sharpened his sense of humor and gave it a uniquely "American" tone and style. These writers and historians tend to accept Will Rogers as the simple country-born humorist and Oklahoma cowboy he always claimed to be. They also tend to view him as a self-made, self-evolving American humorist, the popular culture equivalent of a J. P. Morgan, Ben Franklin, Abraham Lincoln, or other famous, highly successful Americans. These historical figures often proclaimed themselves to be "self-made," even though the records of their respective lives often proved them to be more complicated. In retrospect, they were sometimes considerably different than the myths they constructed about themselves or that were constructed for them.[2]

The fact that many of these Americans played into a variety of cultural myths does not, however, seem to cause any real problems for Will Rogers's many admirers. To them, Will Rogers is the exception to the rule; he is not deliberately casting himself into any cultural myth. Rather, they see him as the real thing—an American phenomenon whose innate sense of humor and unpretentious, down-to-earth cowboy charm and philosophy enabled him naturally and effortlessly to rise in the world. He did this first through the Ziegfeld Follies and later through his work in film, radio, and journalism, until he became one of the most successful and influential men of his time.

These writers and historians also tend to see few meaningful distinctions between Will Rogers, the cultural icon who became a myth and a legend, and Will Rogers, the man who may have been a somewhat different person. For these writers and historians, myth and history are virtually one and the same as they apply to Will Rogers and his life. They view him as the embodiment of many of the cultural myths that Americans have traditionally celebrated in themselves and their country. They also see few, if any, distinctions between Will Rogers the *person*, and Will Rogers the Oklahoma cowboy, a *persona* that may have been cleverly crafted, first for the stage, and later for film, radio, and newspapers.

Examples of these characterizations of Will Rogers are to be found throughout the articles and books that have been written about him since his untimely death in 1935. Donald Day, the editor of *The Autobiography of Will Rogers* (1949), claims that Will Rogers was different than the other "cracker-box philosophers . . . [for] all of them had been one person in private life and another in their character as a horse-sense humorist . . . Will [was] inseparable in his person and in his character as a humorist."[3] Elsewhere, Charles Collins wrote of Will Rogers: "Like America, when Will Rogers started out, a wad of gum in his jaw, twirling a rope, a grin on his face, he didn't know where he was going. His was no planned, educated, groomed, scientifically test-tubed existence. That's why it is so American" (xi).

Others who have written about Will Rogers characterize him in ways that are variations of this same theme. In their book, *A Will Rogers Treasury: Reflection and Observation* (1986), editors Bryan B. Sterling and Frances N. Sterling describe Will Rogers as follows: "Will Rogers was neither a sophisticated actor donning the disguise of a simple cowboy, nor a character invented by a brilliant writer. He was essentially what he seemed—a country boy who had come to the big city."[4] Similarly, in his book *Will Rogers, His Life and Times* (1973), Richard M. Ketchum describes Will Rogers as follows: "With all the fame that came his way, he never really changed. He was exactly what he seemed to be, 'I am just an old country boy in a big town trying to get along,' he once wrote. 'I have been eating pretty regular and the reason I have is, I have stayed an old country boy.'"[5] In a dissertation that was completed in 1958, and later in his book, *Will Rogers* (1974), E. Paul Alworth writes that Will Rogers was the most special of all American humorists because his stage persona was not a "mask" that he could take off or put on whenever it was convenient for him to do so. Rather, he argues that Will Rogers was the most authentic and original of American humorists:

> He fits no convenient category: he was not a rural New England comedian like Jack Downing and Sam Slick; he had no political axe to grind like James Russell Lowell; he had no talent for political vituperation like Petroleum V. Nasby; he did not often play the fool character like Artemus Ward and Bill Nye; he wrote no sustained literature like Mark Twain; and he had no zeal for political and social reform like Martin Dooley.[6]

Alworth concludes that Will Rogers was one of those rare historical figures who occasionally emerge out of a culture, and who legitimately achieve the status of popular icons because they are the living embodiment of everything those cultures value in themselves.

There are others who are less convinced that Will Rogers was simply an Oklahoma cowboy with an innate gift for folksy humor. Nor did they believe Will Rogers the *person*, and Will Rogers the Oklahoma cowboy stage and literary *persona*, were one and the same. These writers believe Will Rogers was a much more sophisticated humorist and satirist than he is often given credit for being. Peter C. Rollins argues in his book, *Will Rogers: A Bio-Bibliography* (1984), that Will Rogers was neither the simple cowboy comedian, nor the self-made humorist perpetuated by his own legend:

> Will Rogers usually approached his audience in the guise of a simple cowboy fresh from the plains of Oklahoma. Contrary to this image, the real Will Rogers grew up in a wealthy, politically dominant family which took a subscription to the *New York Times* (delivered to Oologah by train). Not only were Willie's parents anxious that he amount to something; they were also ready to smooth his way with money and not-so-gentle persuasion. This

> background in part explains how a young man, who claimed only to be a cowboy, eventually became the friendly, perceptive, public critic of the world's most important father figures.[7]

If Rollins is correct and Will Rogers addressed his audience in "the guise of a simple Oklahoma cowboy," then there were clearly considerable differences between Will Rogers the *person*, and Will Rogers the Oklahoma cowboy *persona*.

Elsewhere in his book, Rollins is even more insistent that Will Rogers was a far more sophisticated and worldly individual than was ever apparent in his Oklahoma cowboy stage persona:

> The real Will Rogers was no provincial yokel. Even though he had been an erratic student, he had the equivalent of a high school education; in addition, he had seen much of the world during early ramblings. Letters sent home from South America and Africa reflect an alert mind and a grammatical pen. While on the vaudeville circuit from 1903 to 1908, he wrote a series of some fifty love letters to his fiancé, Betty Blake. These important revelations of his personal feeling . . . show a sophisticated mind at work and bear no relation to the semiliterate diction which Rogers exploited for rhetorical purposes when speaking in this cowboy persona (6).

As Rollins notes, Will Rogers was fully capable of writing "grammatical" prose when he chose to do so, just as he was capable of revealing "a sophisticated mind at work" when it served his purposes. Clearly, then, the semiliterate speech and meanderings of the Oklahoma cowboy persona would have to be the result of both artistic instincts and conscious choices. Very few people who can write grammatically correct prose will do otherwise unless they are trying deliberately to imitate the speech patterns of another character or persona. Will Rogers's ability to write grammatically correct prose is, in many respects, the best evidence we have that the Oklahoma cowboy persona was a deliberate artistic choice. It was also a literary and dramatic creation of the highest order—as acutely reflective of American cultural values as Don Quixote is of Spanish cultural values, or Hamlet is of Danish cultural values, or Dr. Zhivago is of Russian cultural values.

Others are equally convinced that admirers of Will Rogers must be careful to make a distinction between Will Rogers, the man, and Will Rogers, the stage personality. In an introduction to *Will Roger's Weekly Articles, Volume I, The Harding/Coolidge Years: 1922–1925* (1980), editors James M. Smallwood and Steven K. Gragert wrote: "Will Rogers was a man who 'wore many hats,' who led a life filled with variety. He began his career with Wild West shows, performing internationally and billed as the 'Cherokee Kid,' an expert roper."[8]

If Will Rogers "wore many hats," and if he had earlier in his career adopted the identity of the "Cherokee Kid," then he clearly understood the significance of a stage persona. It seems logical to assume that he may have experimented with a variety of such identities, or at least with various manifestations of the Cherokee Kid, before eventually settling on the persona of the Oklahoma cowboy?[9] Will Rogers's early attempts at adopting the Cherokee Kid stage persona, before eventually establishing the Oklahoma cowboy as his stage identity, are very similar to Samuel Clemens's early experiments with various literary pseudonyms before finally adopting "Mark Twain" as his permanent pen name—of which more will be said later.

Homer Croy, who knew Will Rogers personally and wrote a book titled *Our Will Rogers* (1953), describes the problems he confronted when he first took up the challenge of trying to characterize the "real Will Rogers":

> He had been eulogized so ecstatically that I wondered if I could paint him as I saw him—mole and all. There was the vast bulwark of legend that one must go up against; did I dare set the story down as I saw it? One item of the Will Rogers saga was close to the heart of America: 'I never met a man I didn't like.' I knew that this quotation was mostly a happy accident and that in reality there were many men he couldn't abide . . . And I knew also that he had a hot and hasty temper and that he had had two fist fights. As I began to think earnestly of this biography, I asked myself, should I write the traditional Will Rogers story, or the story that I believed to be more nearly true?[10]

Croy's sense that Will Rogers was a remarkably complex individual was reinforced by his own personal experiences with Rogers during the time that they were working together in Hollywood. Croy began to realize that the Oklahoma cowboy was a persona Will Rogers had cleverly and intuitively designed to conceal a far more complex personality:

> During this time, I become better acquainted with Will and began to realize he was not the simple personality that most people assumed. He was, as I began to sense him, a remarkably complex person. His easy, boyish, open approach made people feel that he was just what they saw on the surface. In one sense that was true, but beyond this hail-fellow-well-met personality he was vastly reserved; there was a wall that no one went beyond; and there were dark chambers and hidden recesses that he opened to no one (270–271).

Homer Croy's sense that there were at least two, and perhaps even more versions of "Will Rogers," was also reinforced when he journeyed to Rogers's Oklahoma birthplace to interview the people who had known him best. They described Will Rogers as a far more complicated man than the one presented to the public through the guise of the Oklahoma cowboy:

> I was astonished to find how people disagreed on him. I found that he had many enemies, people who said bitter and acrimonious things about him; some who called him a faker and pretender; and some who found his humor not at all to their liking. Sometimes, as I went from one to another, I could hardly believe they were talking about the same person (ix).

Croy concludes, however, that in spite of these less than favorable impressions of Will Rogers, by the end of his research he realized that he too "loved Will Rogers," as did millions of other Americans (ix).

Anyone who has read the six volumes of *Will Rogers' Weekly Articles* (1980) would have to admit that these are often observations written by a skilled satirist, one who is adept enough to disguise a keen, analytical mind behind the seemingly uneducated utterances of a cowboy-philosopher.[11] Like all skilled satirists, Will Rogers reveals himself in these articles to be a writer of remarkable linguistic sensitivity and self-discipline. These are so carefully honed and controlled that the mask of the Oklahoma cowboy never slips—not even in a single word choice or inappropriate syllable that might inadvertently betray an intelligence and sophistication the writer-actor is trying diligently to conceal.

Will Rogers understood that the least effective way to satirize anything in America is to do so with perfectly constructed, grammatically correct English sentences.[12] Rather, his satire, like all great American satire—including the satirical utterances of Huck Finn in Mark Twain's *Adventures of Huckleberry Finn*—is most effective when it springs up naturally, without apparent effort or intent, from a seemingly illiterate or semiliterate source.

The purpose of this book, *Will Rogers Storyteller*, is thus not to refute his place in American history as a cultural icon. Nor is it to undermine his reputation by suggesting that the Oklahoma cowboy might be as much of a clever literary and stage persona as it is a major force, perhaps *thee* major force in Will Rogers's own personality. His place in American history and the reputation of the Oklahoma cowboy persona are far too secure in the eyes of the American public to ever be seriously challenged by any writer or scholar in the foreseeable future. Nor should they be! Will Rogers justifiably occupies an honored, even revered place in both American popular culture and the hearts of the American people.

I will attempt instead, frequently through direct and indirect references to Will Rogers's personal library, to demonstrate that he is a far more skillful satirist, conscious artist, and intuitive reader of American culture than he has often been given credit for. My hope is this will connect him more directly to other American literary figures and storytellers throughout our history. The purpose is, thus, to paint a somewhat broader, and hopefully richer portrait of Will Rogers. I will also try to demonstrate that the two most brilliant stage and literary personae that evolved out of the deepest wellsprings of American culture and humor, starting with early New England Puritans and extending into the nineteenth and twentieth centuries, are Sam Clemens's "Mark Twain" and Will Rogers's "Oklahoma cowboy."

The following are the issues I will focus on, while making extensive use of the books in his own library.

- Will Rogers as a product of early twentieth-century American historical trends and demographic changes.
- Will Rogers as an extension of the historical and cultural traditions of the early New England Puritans, eighteenth-century colonial humorists (especially Ben Franklin), and nineteenth-century frontier humorists.
- Will Rogers's personal life and career, especially his early years in vaudeville, to determine to what extent he is part of the distinguished tradition of American stage humorists and satirists.
- Will Rogers's relationship to Mark Twain—the dominant American humorists of the nineteenth and twentieth centuries.
- Will Rogers as an intuitively instinctive, yet deliberately conscious artist who discusses his craft and his artistry quite openly, albeit somewhat factiously, in essays such as "The Extemporaneous Line" and "How to be Funny."
- Will Rogers as a performer who understood better than others of his time how the electronic media would shape the future of entertainment.
- Will Rogers's role as a dedicated humanitarian and advocate for the world's poor and hungry.
- Will Rogers as a writer and author, especially in the context of his personal library and newspaper articles.
- The connections between the Will Rogers's storytelling tradition and other earlier trends in the development of American humor.

I will also try to explain the personal connection I felt with him at the end of the last century when I roamed around his ranch house and adjacent property, sat for hours reading the books in his library, and walked among the furniture and mementos that surrounded him in his daily life.

As the flames consumed his ranch on January 7, 2025, I remembered thinking that he still had so much to tell us before his life ended tragically at the age of fifty-five in Point Barrow, Alaska. With the ranch now gone, those memories needed to be communicated to a younger generation, many of whom probably would not even recognize his name. Whether he was Will Rogers, the Oklahoma cowboy, or both, his message that humor can be a great healer and provide insights into our common humanity may be more important than ever before.

What emerges will hopefully be a broader view of Will Rogers and the Oklahoma cowboy. He may have been such a skilled and sophisticated artist and satirist that the American public, even long after his death, has yet to fully appreciate the man behind the myth, the humorist behind his stage personality, and the artist behind the cowboy-philosopher.

---

1. The direct and indirect references in this book to the "Will Rogers Library" are to the books that are stored in the Will Rogers State Historic Park in Santa Monica, California. The library contains approximately 2,600 volumes, which are stored in three places in Will Rogers's former home. Will's personal books, and books relating to his life and times, are stored in the main library. The California State Parks inventoried the library in 1944, 1949, 1959, and 1970, and I am indebted to them for the information these inventories provided for this book. A significant number of the books in Will Rogers's personal library were sent to him by his many fans and admirers, as well as by authors and publishers. Will Rogers himself apparently acquired very few books, and the extent to which he read and used his personal library is debatable, although the physical evidence suggests that he may have used these books occasionally as reference tools. Other books are underlined and/or contain marginal notations which indicate more extensive use. However, as I attempted to establish the cultural, historical, and literary antecedents for both Will Rogers and his Oklahoma cowboy persona through a variety of sources, including the books in his own personal library, I established several broad, general guidelines for my own research. They are as follows: 1) any attempt to connect Will Rogers's stage, film, and literary careers to his readings involves few certainties and much more in the way of intelligent speculation based on the available evidence; 2) Will Rogers probably did not read many of the books sent to him by his fans, authors, and publishers—he seems, instead, to have accepted these books more out of politeness than out of any desire to read them, although at times their subject matters

were undoubtedly of interest to him; 3) the specific types of books that were sent to him nonetheless demonstrate how strongly the American public associated Will Rogers with certain themes, including the original frontier, western cowboy traditions, aviation, world politics, etc.; 4) the mere fact that so many different people sent books to Will Rogers suggests that a significant number of Americans viewed him as being somewhat more sophisticated than the semiliterate Oklahoma cowboy he claimed to be; 5) some books in the main library—especially those with worn bindings, underlined texts, and/or marginal notations—provide significant evidence that these volumes may have been used by Will Rogers in the preparation of his newspaper articles and other stage, film, and literary activities; and 6) any evidence whatsoever that Will Rogers used his personal library even sporadically—and such evidence does exist—is sufficient reason to take with a grain of salt his many statements that he did not have much faith in "book learning." This rejection of "book learning" seems instead to be a necessary element in the development of this Oklahoma cowboy persona.

2. Richard Hofstadter, *Anti-intellectualism in America Life* (New York: Alfred A. Knopf, 1970) 253.
3. Donald Day, "Foreword," *The Autobiography of Will Rogers* (Boston: Houghton Mifflin Company, 1949) xv.
4. Bryan B. Frances N. Sterling, "Introduction," *A Will Rogers Treasury* (New York: Bonanza Books, 1982) 3.
5. Richard M, Ketchum, *Will Rogers, His Life and Times* (New York: American Heritage Publishing Company, Inc.: 1973) 7.
6. E. Paul Alworth, *Will Rogers* (New York: Twayne Publishers, 1974) 124.
7. Peter C. Rollins, *Will Rogers: A Bio-Bibliography* (Westport Connecticut: Greenwood Press 1984) 3–4.
8. James M. Smallwood and Steven K. Gragert, "Introduction," *Will Rogers' Weekly Articles*, Vol. I (Stillwater, Oklahoma: Oklahoma State University Press, 1980) xiii.
9. See Peter C. Rollins discussion of the "cowboy persona" (3–6, 8, 126–127); the "Cherokee Kid" persona (162); and the "Jubilo persona" (178–179, 182, 184, 187–188, 197, 200).
10. Homer Croy, *Our Will Rogers* (Boston: Little, Brown and Company, 1953) vii.
11. The six volumes of *Will Rogers' Weekly Articles* were edited by James M. Smallwood and Steven K. Gragert, and they were published by the Oklahoma State University Press in Stillwater, Oklahoma, in 1980. These six volumes contain the complete writings of Will Rogers during the time that he wrote a nationally syndicated newspaper column from December of 1922 until his death in August of 1935.
12. See Walter Blair's discussion of the emerging "language" of the "frontier" or "southwestern" humorists in his classic study *Native American Humor* (1800–1900). San Francisco: Chandler Publishing Company, Inc.: 1937) 91–92.

# II.

# COUNTRY BOY IN THE CITY

THROUGHOUT HIS life, Will Rogers demonstrated a remarkable ability to utilize the emerging technologies of virtually all forms of the mass media to perpetuate his own evolving legend. He was quick to recognize and exploit the many opportunities created by the new technologies of film and radio. Together with his work as a newspaper columnist, film and radio gave him access to virtually every form of mass media that was available to entertainers in the early part of the twentieth century. Perhaps more than any other popular entertainer of his time, he understood the awesome powers of these new forms of communication and entertainment. As Peter Rollins writes, "in the Follies period the lasso fit around the island of Manhattan, but as Rogers explored print and electronic media, the loop would eventually surround every American who attended a movie, listened to a radio, or read a morning newspaper" (6).

Will Rogers became involved in films, and later radio, at a time when other established entertainers were avoiding these highly risky enterprises. Many veteran stage entertainers, of whom Will Rogers was one, had reservations about the movie industry. They were wary of the fact that their voices, an indispensable part of their acting skills on stage, would not be heard on films. For these veteran entertainers, the "silence" of the "silent films" was a disadvantage that they believed would prove to be professionally suicidal. They also believed the "silence" of these films would make it impossible for movies to ever seriously compete with traditional stage entertainment. They believed films without sound were most likely a temporary fad that would soon disappear from the American scene, once again restoring traditional stage acting to its rightful place in the entertainment hierarchy.[1]

Will Rogers, however, seemed to recognize almost immediately that films, even the silent films and radio, were the new national "stages" for entertainers, and they would soon replace the antiquated stages of the Ziegfeld Follies and other such regional theaters. He seemed to have an intuitive sense that whatever disadvantages the silent films might present for veteran stage entertainers, those disadvantages were far surpassed by the simple fact that an entertainer on film would reach a much larger audience. In this sense, Will Rogers displayed an uncanny ability to identify the advantages of this new popular storytelling form long before many of his contemporary entertainers were even aware of its power. This is a significant accomplishment for the simple, poorly educated, unworldly Oklahoma cowboy he played on stage, and which some of his admirers insist is the "real Will Rogers."

According to the *Chronicle of America* (1990) by Clifton Daniel, "movies," or "flickers," had established themselves as "one of the biggest things in the entertainment industry" as early as the year 1896.[2] By the year 1903, the "peep shows" and "flickers" were gradually being replaced by films such as *The Great Train Robbery*, an "epic of nearly 12 minutes," which introduced hitherto unknown elements into films—plot and narrative continuity (*Chronicle*, 540). It wasn't until the late 1920s that film producers began to experiment seriously with sound. By that time, Will Rogers had already been involved in films for over a decade. As Byron B. and Frances N. Sterling point out in their book *Will Rogers in Hollywood* (1984), he appeared in over sixty movies from 1918 until his death in 1935. Some of these films Rogers scripted himself, as he had done with some earlier scripts for the Ziegfeld Follies.[3]

As for the quality of Will Rogers's work in these early films, Bryan B. and Frances N. Sterling argue that this Oklahoma cowboy was a first-rate film talent:

> We also learned in the course of this research that the long- believed myth that Will Rogers was unsuccessful in his silent films—handed down from writer to writer like a treasured legend—was just that, a myth. Nothing could be farther from fact. Artistically and critically, those silent films were acclaimed. *One Glorious Day* was chosen the foremost motion picture of 1922 by the National Board of

> Review—tantamount to today's Academy Award as best picture of the year (Hollywood, ix).

If Will Rogers was nothing more than a simple Oklahoma cowboy, he certainly displayed his lack of worldly sophistication in a most interesting way, for he played a central role in a movie that won an award that would be the equivalent of today's Academy Award for best film.

Since Will Rogers appeared in over sixty movies, he clearly had the ability to adapt to a variety of different roles and characters. He didn't always play himself in these films, although some of his roles are variations of the Oklahoma cowboy, whereas others are radical departures from this stage persona. Peter Rollins acknowledges that although Will Rogers was "first cast as a cowboy," he eventually created a "second film persona" that was radically different from either the earlier Oklahoma cowboy persona, or the later philosopher-statesman persona:

> After a short time as a cowboy, Rogers developed a second film persona. Called "Jubilo," this figure is a rural clown, a perpetual loafer who floats through society getting himself into trouble and avoiding work whenever possible. Jubilo is an eccentric figure whom we love despite his numerous flaws. He is distinctly unlike the later philosophical Rogers' persona: Jubilo can fall in love and even has a few (rather athletic) fistfights (54).

Will Rogers, through his work in films, revealed himself to be an entertainer who was capable of wearing many hats and playing many different roles. It is also possible that early in his career he recognized the changing interests of the American entertainment audience. Perhaps he realized that many displaced country people were forced to relocate to our nation's cities in the early part of the twentieth century. Could that insight have enabled him to develop the Oklahoma cowboy persona, and later his various film personae, to accommodate the changing interests and emotional needs of his audience?

By the year 1920, as Will Rogers's reputation was rapidly transcending the Ziegfeld Follies and exploding onto the national scene through his films, there were some dramatic demographic changes taking place in America. As reported in the *Chronicle of America* (1990), by the year 1920 more and more farm families were being uprooted and moved to the nation's cities. This created an urban population of displaced people who had been raised in the country, with country values, but who were trying desperately to adjust to the complexities of city life:

> The census this year shows a population of 105,710,620, and a general urbanization of the nation. Less than half of those people live in the country, as the urban environment continues to seduce the rural population. The number of farm residents in America has fallen below 30 percent of the overall population (612).

Small wonder that the Oklahoma cowboy stage personality would find a ready-made audience of displaced country folk who could easily identify with, and perhaps be seduced by, statements such as, "I am just an old country boy in a big town trying to get along . . . I have been eating pretty regular and the reason I have is, I have stayed an old country boy."[4]

Will Rogers understood very early in his career the type of people who would comprise his audiences, and how specifically he might reach these displaced individuals and families. America itself had become a nation of country people "in a big town trying to get along." The American people, or at least a significant percentage of them who had been born and raised on farms or in rural communities, were struggling to adjust to city life. They often clung desperately to their country values, for they provided the only security these displaced individuals were to know in an urban environment that was becoming increasingly insecure and complex. The stage for an Oklahoma cowboy comedian was set not merely by the Ziegfeld Follies, but also by the shifting historical trends and demographic patterns that were creating dramatic changes in the fabric of American life in the early decades of the twentieth century.

There are other ways in which Will Rogers's appeal and success were products of historical trends that were taking place in the twentieth century. Like Elvis Presley, a cultural icon who arrived on the national scene in the middle of the same century, Will Rogers arrived on the national scene at a time when electronic technologies had advanced to the point where entertainers could transcend their regions or locales and literally be invited into the nation's homes. Elvis Presley had a ready-made audience of post-adolescent teenagers who were the products of the World War II baby boom. He was able to tap into that audience on the national level through the relatively recent invention of television, which allowed for him to enter the nation's homes through *The Ed Sullivan Show* and *The Steve Allen Show*. Perhaps, more than anything else, this accounts for Elvis Presley's rapid rise from regional entertainer to national entertainer, and eventually to cultural icon.

A similar phenomenon can partially explain Will Rogers's dramatic transcendence from regional entertainer to cultural icon. His potential audience was extremely large. A significant percentage of the American population in the early part of the twentieth century was comprised of country-born and -raised individuals who had migrated to our nation's cities. The challenge was, "How could an entertainer reach such a large audience?" Certainly, the Ziegfeld Follies, even when it toured the country, could only reach a very small percentage of these people. Will Rogers was shrewd enough to tap into and utilize to his advantage virtually every new technology that would provide him with a national forum or a national stage on which he could reach this massive audience.

Although in 1920 there were only two thousand radios in American homes, by January 1, 1924, there were 2.5 million radios in these same homes (*Chronicle*, 624). Four years later, on January 4, 1928, the "National Broadcasting Company link[ed] all 48 states to hear radio extravaganzas with stars such as Will Rogers and Al Jolson" (*Chronicle*, 638). Thus, four short years after the number of American homes with radios had increased from two thousand to more than 2.5 million, Will Rogers found a way to reach a potentially massive audience in all forty-eight states. We must once again recognize his uncanny ability to become intimately involved in another form of mass media at the very moment when its power was about to be unleashed on a massive nationwide audience.

Newspapers certainly were not new to the American scene when Will Rogers began to write for them in 1926. Nor was writing a completely new vocation for him, for he had already written some scripts for both film and stage. He took to writing a newspaper column as naturally as he had adapted to his radio shows or film roles (Rollins, 35–37). He always had an extremely sophisticated sense of what would appeal to a newspaper-reading audience. Referring to the way he had used newspaper material on stage, he stated in his essay, "The Extemporaneous Line," that "the more up-to-date a subject is the more credit you are given for talking on it."[5] He understood that the more contemporary his material (i.e., newspaper material), the less funny his delivery had to be, whereas with "old subject[s], your gags must be funny to get over" (35–37). These observations, which he made in 1917, reflect a mind that consciously, deliberately and instinctively sized-up his audience to maximize his entertainment appeal. This awareness also enabled him to make a relatively simple transition from the time when he used newspapers for his stage material to the time when he actually began to write for them.

As Homer Croy writes in *Our Will Rogers* (1953), Rogers decided very early in his newspaper career to write his column in his own unique, inimitable speaking style because he believed this style would appeal to the largest possible audience (182). Recognizing the relatively short attention span of the average American reader, he decided to keep his column short, no more than "125 to 150 words" (183). Furthermore, he chose to adopt a telegram-style partly out of necessity, since during his travels he wired his columns back to his newspaper editors. This turned out to be a brilliant decision, for he understood that the average American reader had limited reading time and would probably prefer something that could be read quickly. In most of his columns, he also allowed his mind to meander around the subtleties of the subject matter, while he developed a series of short, pithy commentaries and humorous observations rather than the traditional one or two punch lines favored by many newspaper columnists. Utilizing the same technique future stand-up comedians such as Bob Hope or Johnny Carson would adopt, he realized if any of his humorous observations fell flat, they would not destroy the whole piece. The reader would soon have other humorous observations to chuckle over.

All of these rhetorical choices reflect a sophisticated mind, one that was well aware of the idiosyncrasies of his audience—common Americans of average educational backgrounds who comprised the nation's radio and newspaper audiences. He also understood that the average readers of his column could probably identify more closely with his colloquial, vernacular style than they could with a style that was grammatically correct to the point of tediousness. And he was aware that these same average American readers would probably not be interested in intellectually stimulating arguments, but would rather prefer some down-to-earth common sense and good country humor in both style and content. Long before the term "sound bite" was even coined, he knew his readers would probably remember his column, and they would come back to it again and again because of some short, pithy statement that was easy for them to remember and relate to their friends. This way they appeared to be retelling a good joke that had been told to them by an intimate acquaintance.

As we review Will Rogers's involvement in newspapers and the electronic media, it seems clear that he had an instinctive ability to identify the largest possible audience for his form of entertainment. He also had the ability to subtly redefine or modify his stage personality to appeal to this audience. And he was able to identify and utilize the three forums—film, radio, and newspapers—that would provide him with the most effective ways of reaching this audience.

Without this national exposure, there undoubtedly would still have been a Will Rogers. It is questionable, however, if he would have achieved the status of cultural icon. A significant part of his talent was not only his ability to refine and modify his stage personality, but also his ability to market it for the largest possible national audience. A man who had this much business acumen, and this much sensitivity to his audience, would also have the ability to create a stage and literary persona of the Oklahoma cowboy that he would use on a variety of national stages throughout his life.

---

1. See Lewis Jacob's *The Rise of the American Film* (New York: Teachers College Press, 1968) 59 and 127–128. Jacobs points out that by the year 1908, "most of the directors, actors, and cameramen who had come to the movies were more or less ashamed of their connection with them . . . Nearly everyone still regarded movie making as a shabby occupation" According to Jacobs, these doubts about film careers lingered well into the next decade, when many actors and actresses were concerned about "The question that had worried them the most was, 'Would pictures hurt a stage career?'" Will Rogers was not, of course, the first stage actor to go

into films, but he was certainly in the forefront of the more successful stage actors who gave up careers in legitimate theater to join the far more risky film production companies.

2. Clifton Daniel, ed., *Chronicle of America* (Mount Kisco, New York: Prentice Hall Trade, 1990) 513.
3. Bryan B. and Frances N. Sterling, *Will Rogers in Hollywood* (New York: Crown Publishers, Inc., 1984) v-x.
4. Richard M. Ketchum, *Will Rogers, His Life and Times* (New York: American Heritage Publishing Company, 1973) 7.
5. Will Rogers, "The Extemporaneous Line," "*How To Be Funny" & other writings of Will Rogers*, ed. Steven K. Gragert (Stillwater, Oklahoma: Oklahoma State University Press, 1983) 3.

# III.

# PURITANISM AND AMERICAN HUMOR

LIKE CHARLIE Chaplin's film character of the Tramp, who was frequently portrayed as a displaced loner attempting to adjust to the complexities of city life in the early decades of the twentieth century, so too Will Rogers's stage and literary persona of the Oklahoma cowboy was a product of his own unique time and place in American history. Still, this stage and literary persona may also have had its roots in the earliest decades of the American experience in the New World.

Whoever created the aphorism, "The more things change, the more they remain the same," could easily have been describing Will Rogers in the context of the American humorists who came before him. His style, delivery, and many of his subject matters would have been recognized by earlier American humorists. The major differences were simply that Will Rogers had a larger national audience and was less distinguishable from his public persona than were most of these early American humorists. As Walter Blair and Hamlin Hill point out in their book *America's Humor* (1978), although Will Rogers has antecedents among the earlier American humorists, his uniqueness was due to the fact that he "was the first great cowboy comedian to come along."[1]

This raises several questions. Was Will Rogers truly an "original," or was he the inevitable extension of the colonial satirists who sprang up in the New World a century after the Puritans arrived on these shores? If Will Rogers *is* an extension of this satirical tradition, what are its ultimate sources in American culture? What precisely is "American humor," and how does Will Rogers's satire reflect the deepest wellsprings of that tradition? These are some of the questions Will Rogers's humor and satire raise when we attempt to establish his place within the full sweep and scope of American cultural history.

Many of Will Rogers's admirers insist that the Oklahoma cowboy's satire is American humor in its purest form. They are convinced that Will Rogers was in touch with the untarnished core of American culture, and he tied together more of the disparate elements of American humor than any other of our nation's great humorists, with the exception of Mark Twain. However, Twain's humor lacked the optimistic spirit that was so closely associated with the New World experience. This optimism is far more evident in Will Rogers's gentler, more upbeat satire than it is in Mark Twain's darker, more brooding satire and humor. This is especially true in Twain's later works such as *The Mysterious Stranger* (1916) and *Letters from the Earth* (1962).

The authentic "American" quality of Will Rogers and his humor has been recognized by his many readers and admirers. Damon Runyon described him as follows:

> Will Rogers was America's most complete human document. He reflected in many ways the heartbeat of America. In thought and manner of appearance and in this daily life he was probably our most typical native born, the closest living approach to what we like to call the true American.[2]

Similarly, Franklin Delano Roosevelt said of Will Rogers, "There was something infectious about his humor. His appeal went straight to the heart of the nation."[3] Peter Rollins, author of *Will Rogers A Bio-Bibliography* (1984), strikes a similar chord when he writes, "Will Rogers meant so much to his people in a time of change and deprivation because he presented them with an image of what America had been told to believe was the best in their national character"(72). Homer Croy agrees when he writes that Will Rogers "was a typical American . . . [and yet he was] truly a great, magnificent American" (328).

If Will Rogers understood and practiced "American humor" better than any of his contemporaries, how then do we define this humor and what are its earliest sources?

As we search for the sources of American humor (i.e., Will Rogers's humor), we inevitably find ourselves in a predicament similar to that of the early explorers who searched for the source of the Mississippi River. Each time these explorers thought they had found the source, they soon realized they had only discovered another of its tributaries. These explorers had to journey farther and farther north as they tried to distinguish the main source of the Mississippi River from its many tributaries.

The same is true for those who search for the sources of American humor, and more specifically the sources of Will Rogers's humor, in our nation's past. Each time one connects Will Rogers's humor to various literary and cultural traditions—western novels, early American storytelling traditions, mainstream American satire, vaudeville, the frontier tall tale, etc.—it soon becomes apparent that most of these are tributaries. They are not the main source.

We must inevitably search deeper into our nation's past to locate the ultimate cultural and historical sources of Will Rogers's understated, intuitive genius. Some of those tributaries, perhaps even the main river, inevitably take us back to the earliest years of the American experience in the New World.

Will Rogers would undoubtedly have raised an eyebrow and gently looked askance at anyone who suggested that his humor was connected to the early Puritans. Still, there is some validity to such an assertion, even though on the surface the argument might seem difficult to make. He seems about as unlikely a descendant of the earlier Puritans as another world-renowned satirist whose deeply religious mother was steeped in theology and the Bible. Yet, this is precisely what happened to Mark Twain, as we shall see later. To be sure, Rogers was not as directly connected to the theology of the early Puritans. Still, it is impossible to live in America and not feel the influence of the Puritans. They created our earliest culture, and we all still live in it.

As far as we know, there were no Puritan humorists or satirists in either the Plymouth Plantation (1620) or Massachusetts Bay (1628) colonies.[4] They undoubtedly had every reason to be stern and grim-faced as they struggled for their very survival on a continent with very few of the essentials that sustain life. Nonetheless, the ideas they brought with them to the New World had much to do with the shaping of both our national character and eventually our sense of humor.

Reverend H. R. Haweis, in his book *American Humorists* (1882), wrote: "The Pilgrims were far too grim and grave to joke; but their descendants, who are fully alive to their peculiarities and weaknesses, while inheriting a full share of both, are not so particular."[5] Similarly, Andrew Lang writes in *Lost Leaders* (1889) that our national humorists, whatever they might appear to be on the surface, are nonetheless often so familiar with religious ideas and the Bible that they are "Puritans at the bottom, as well as rustics."[6]

Constance Rourke, author of *American Humor: A Study of the National Character* (1931), disagrees. She writes that it is easy to locate many "Yankee strength[s]" in the early Puritans, but it is extremely difficult to locate their sense of humor:

> As the texture of Puritan life is examined, sources of Yankee strength become apparent, but not of Yankee humor; for humor is a matter of fantasy, and the fantasies of the Puritan, viewed with the most genial eye, remain sufficiently dark . . . Between these many shadows and the persistent humor of the Yankee the gulf seems wide (19–20).

Rourke argues, however, that we must not judge the Puritans by their outwardly stoic, seemingly unemotional exteriors. Rather, she points out that "emotion was pervasive in New England" (20). Since the Puritans had to suppress those emotions, they undoubtedly developed an acute awareness of the incongruities and ironic juxtapositions between the way they had to appear to feel for the sake of propriety and decorum, and the way they actually felt about many things. Rourke concludes that these experiences may very well have provided the foundations for what later became a unique form of American humor (20–21).

The original New England Puritans were, at least in their public lives, an apparently grim, serious group of men and women who tended to associate humor and levity with something evil, satanic, or morally corrupt. In their private lives, the Puritans may have been a much less rigid and austere group, but publicly they had little tolerance for mirth and levity.

Even to a latter-day descendant of the early Puritans like Nathaniel Hawthorne, who wrote his novels and short stories about his ancestors in the middle of the nineteenth century, laughter was frequently used to foreshadow some sinful event or morally inappropriate decision a literary character was about to make.[7] In one of his short stories, a young character named "Robin" goes on a journey in search of his "kinsman" in a small New England community, only to learn that his relative is a colonial governor who has been tarred and feathered and is being carried out of town on a rail. At first Robin is perplexed as the townspeople laugh and applaud the humiliation of his kinsman. Then, slowly, Robin "sent forth a shout of laughter that echoed through the street . . . every man shook his sides, every man emptied his lungs, but Robin's shout was the loudest there."

In another of Hawthorne's short stories, a character named Ethan Brand goes in search of the "unpardonable sin," only to find it exists in his own cruel, overly intellectualized heart. At the very moment that Ethan has this revelation, he breaks "into a laugh of scorn . . . a slow heavy laugh." Almost immediately the omniscient author comments, "Laughter, when out of place, mistimed, or bursting forth from a disordered state of feeling, may be the most terrible modulation of the human voice."

To the Puritans, laughter was not considered a healthy release of emotional energy or response to any experience. It was a sign of submission to the darker forces in human nature. So how did humor ever evolve in a Puritan culture that often regarded laughter itself, especially public laughter, as a sign of moral weakness or degradation?

The closest thing we have to a humorist or satirist in the early New England colonies is perhaps Thomas Morton, the author of *New England Canaan* (1632). However, Morton does not necessarily qualify as an "American" humorist because he had only a superficial and sporadic attachment to the Massachusetts Bay and Plymouth Plantation colonies. Nonetheless, his occasionally satirical, anti-establishment commentaries on the New England Puritans and their values foreshadow the types of humor that will eventually flow from the pens of Mark Twain and Will Rogers. Of his early experiences in the New World, Morton writes:

> In the year since the carnation of Christ, 1622, it was my chance to be landed in the parts of New England, where I found two sortes of

> people, the one Christian, the other infidels, these I found most full of humanity, and more friendly than the other . . .[8]

The New England Puritans, who were the butt of jokes occasionally directed at them by Thomas Morton and the more remote European satirists, were nonetheless instrumental in the development of American humor, even though they seemingly had no sense of humor, and apparently wrote no humor or satire. When the original Puritans left England for the New World, they not only reduced themselves in status to the level of "commoners," at least by European standards. They also placed themselves outside the political, economic, social, and artistic spheres of the European establishment and cultural elite.[9] By doing so, they eventually established the perspective that future American satirists and humorists would consistently use to their advantage: the perspective of a disadvantaged, often lower-class outsider satirizing a world controlled by a privileged upper class.

Once they arrived in the New World, the Puritans at first seemed indifferent to events in Europe, primarily because they were preoccupied with a multitude of problems—famine, disease, natural disasters, etc.—that confronted them daily. Later, when they became increasingly aware of the deprivations of their New England lifestyles, they occasionally cast an envious eye in the direction of Europe. In time, this was accompanied by a growing awareness that they lived in a culturally inferior environment, a fact that is painfully obvious in poems such as Anne Bradstreet's "The Author to her Book." In this poem, she expresses her profound embarrassment over a book of her poems, *The Tenth Muse* (1650), which was published in Europe without her knowledge. Acknowledging the inferior quality of her own work when judged by European standards, Anne Bradstreet compares her book of poems to a "rambling brat" that is "unfit" for public consumption.[10]

In time, however, the second- and third-generation Puritan communities became feistier about their own predicament in the New World. Eventually, they became outwardly defiant toward the European establishment that made its arrogant, superior presence felt in their lives through political and economic domination. Eventually, these early Puritan communities, existing as they did on the edge of deprivation and poverty, began to look rather scornfully at the pretentiousness of the European establishment and cultural elite. With this shift in the New England colonies' attitudes toward Europe, we can begin to recognize the germinating seed of American humor—a seed that would burst forth with a multitude of eighteenth- and nineteenth-century satirists and humorists. Indeed, America would virtually become a nation of humorists who grew out of the seemingly unlikely soil of the early Puritan colonies in the New World (Rourke, 19–21).

Although at first the Puritans and their direct descendants addressed their feelings toward Europe and its ruling classes in the most serious of tones and styles, they nonetheless succeeded in establishing the point of view that would eventually dominate American humor. This was the point of view of the commoner or lower-class character, living on the edge of deprivation and poverty, who passes judgment on the pretentious, frequently hypocritical and exploitative values of the establishment. Substitute *humorous* or *satirical* commentaries for the Puritans' more serious statements regarding what they perceived to be the failings of the European establishment, and we have the arena in which later American humorists such as Mark Twain and Will Rogers would exercise their considerable satirical skills.

Even though they wrote no humor or satire, the Puritans' experiences in the New World thus established the foundations for an American humor and satire that would eventually be much different than that of our British and other European neighbors. The British satirists were often members of a cultural elite who frequently wrote satire to express their disdain for the coarse, vulgar tastes and values of common or lower-class people. Even William Shakespeare, although he attributes much levity and mirth to his common or lower-class characters, often reserves his most caustic wit to satirize their vulgar tastes and values. This is true, for example, of the gravedigger in *Hamlet*, the servants Speed and Launce in *Two Gentlemen of Verona*, the shipwrecked crew in *The Tempest*, the drunken Falstaff in *King Henry IV*, or other such characters.[11]

American satirists such as Will Rogers, on the other hand, normally adopt the point of view of a common or lower-class character expressing his or her opinions of the pretentious, exploitative, elitist values and lifestyles of the ruling upper class. This generalization does not always hold true, but in the broadest possible terms, the role of the speaker and the role of the victim of the satire are frequently reversed in British/European and American satire. Undoubtedly, this pattern can be traced all the way back to the situation the Puritans found themselves in once they arrived in the New World, where they were suddenly cast in the roles of commoners or outsiders.

There are other ways in which the early New England Puritans inadvertently established the foundations of American humor—and eventually for Will Rogers's humor—even though they wrote no humor or satire themselves. The Puritans, who seemingly had no sense of humor and seldom revealed their emotions, are the logical cultural source for the many "dead-pan comedians" such as Buster Keaton, or "poker-faced reporters" such as Mark Twain who eventually dominated our national stage. Twain even argues in an essay titled "How to Tell a Story" that the American storyteller "does his best to conceal the fact that he even dimly suspects that there is anything funny about it."[12]

The traditions of deadpan comedy and poker-faced reporting must have had a cultural antecedent somewhere. Could it be the Puritans, who so seldom laughed on the outside, were sometimes laughing on the inside? Was this the beginnings of deadpan humor and poker-faced reporting? We also sense in the Puritans' predicament in the New World the beginnings of what eventually became almost a national obsession with stage and literary "personae." Because the Puritans were not allowed to reveal how they truly felt about some of the absurdities and hypocrisies that surrounded them, perhaps they had to adopt public personae that concealed their innermost feelings.

It is clear in some of the early Puritan writings, especially those that were never meant to be exposed to public scrutiny, that the early Puritans frequently had private lives that were significantly different than their public lives. Some of them become master actors and actresses, people who were remarkably skilled at assuming public personae to disguise and conceal their private feelings and emotions. This conflict can be seen in the private writings of Anne Bradstreet (1612–1672) and Edward Taylor (1642–1729).

Bradstreet wrote poems such as "The Flesh and the Spirit," in which the speaker sounds like the traditional Puritan who uses heavy-handed allegory to condemn the sinful side of human nature that succumbs too easily to the temptations of the flesh. But she also wrote poems such as "To My Dear and Loving Husband," "Before the Birth of One of Her Children," and other such poems, which reveal her to be a woman of great emotional depths and even sensuality.

Her poem, "Verses Upon the Burning of Our House," reveals the basic conflict between the private person and the public persona that the Puritans were forced to contend with daily. In this poem, the speaker assumes the public persona of the orthodox Puritan who attempts to accept the loss of her home by arguing that since it was God's Will, she as a mere mortal has no choice but to accept her loss and bless "His name that gave and took." However, in the fourth stanza of the poem, the public persona suddenly drops completely, revealing a more private person, one who is attempting to cope with many different human emotions, including grief, loss, sentimentality, and a profound sense of nostalgia for her earthly possessions:

When by the ruins oft I passed
My sorrowing eyes aside did cast,
And here and there the places spy
Where oft I sat, and long did lie.

Here stood that trunk, and there that chest;
There lay that store I counted best;
My pleasant things in ashes lie,
And them behold no more shall I.

Similarly, Edward Taylor, an early Puritan pastor of a church in Westfield, Massachusetts, wrote private poems to examine various theological issues, which he would then use as the foundations for his sermons. However, none of Taylor's contemporaries were apparently even aware that he wrote poetry. Until the discovery of these poems in the 1930s, most historians and scholars assumed that Edward Taylor was simply the orthodox, even conservative minister he had appeared to be throughout his life. The poems, however, reveal a very different person concealed behind the public persona of the Puritan minister.

In his private poems, Taylor imitated the more humorous and satirical poetic styles of the British metaphysical poets such as John Donne and George Herbert. As a result, his poetry contains earthy images and language that are occasionally sensual, incongruous, erotic, scatological, and even humorous. In "The Preface" to a long poem titled *God's Determinations Concerning his Elect*, Taylor, with apparently deliberate incongruity, compares the biblical creation to what might have taken place in some celestial "Bowling Alley," with God being the Supreme Bowler and the "Sun" being his bowling ball. Whether Taylor meant for this analogy to be taken seriously or humorously is unknown. What is clear is the visual image of God bowling in a celestial bowling alley, using the sun as a bowling ball, is one the tall tale storytellers of a later generation would love for its humorous effect—not its theological implications.

Humorous, deliberately incongruous images like this suggest that the early Puritans had private and public lives that were significantly different. These private writings also suggest that the early Puritans were masters of public personae. They were quite possibly the ultimate source of the multitude of stage and literary personae created by the eighteenth-century colonial satirists and nineteenth-century frontier humorists.

We must also remember that the original Puritans were the first "escape artists" in a country that eventually became, during the frontier phase in American history (1803–1890), a nation of people who fled or escaped into the West. The precedent for this was undoubtedly established by the original Puritans when they broke from the Church of England because they believed it had become "too Catholic," which was a euphemistic way of saying it had become too decadent, too corrupt, and too "civilized" in the negative sense of the term (Parrington, 3–15). Thus, the Puritans established one of the most popular motifs in all of American literature and popular culture: the journey out of a decadent, corrupt, overly civilized world and into a new frontier.

The Puritans did not idealize their pilgrimage to the New World, as would some American writers during the frontier phase of our national history. The Puritans saw America as a "heathen wilderness," which William Bradford, governor of Plymouth Plantation, described as "those vast and unpeopled countries of America, which are fruitful and fit for habitation, being devoid of all civil inhabitants, where there are only savage and brutish men which range up and down, little otherwise than the wild beasts of the same."[13] Even though the Puritans did not idealize the New World, they played a significant role in establishing the journey-motif as one of the guiding metaphors, perhaps *thee* guiding metaphor, in all of American culture. As Janice Stout speculates in her book, *The Journey Narrative in American Literature* (1983), "American literature is . . . obsessed with journeys, possibly to an even greater degree than has been supposed."[14]

We should note that much American humor, including the newspaper columns Will Rogers wrote during his many travels, involves writers or protagonists who go on journeys in which they are forced to confront the idiosyncrasies of foreign cultures or local traditions. Will Rogers and Mark Twain, together with numerous other American humorists, were virtually obsessive and compulsive travelers. Many of their best literary efforts were written during their journeys to foreign countries. Indeed, our nation's humorists have traditionally been fascinated by journeys—either their own journeys, or those they have established for their literary personae. This, too, must have an antecedent somewhere in our national history, perhaps even in New England Puritanism and continuing into the frontier era of westward expansion.

Although the Puritans consistently read the King James Bible and other religious treatises, they were "anti-intellectual" and "anti-book learning" to the extent that they strongly disapproved of literature and virtually every other form of human discourse that was not practical, or that did not have a religious or moral purpose. They felt that everything humans needed to know to live meaningful lives could be found in the Bible. In their opinion, if it wasn't in the Bible, then it probably wasn't worth knowing. The only exception was writing that had a functional or practical purpose. This is why our early poets—Anne Bradstreet, Michael Wigglesworth, and Edward Taylor—were so self-conscious about their respective crafts. They had been conditioned by their culture to believe that poetry was neither practical nor moral.

Richard Hofstadter, in his book *Anti-Intellectualism in American Thought*, points out that nothing is more American—and perhaps nothing so symptomatic of a culture that is rooted in the original Puritan experience in the New World—than this anti-intellectual bias against books.[15] When Will Rogers satirizes "book learning" and celebrates experience as a learning tool, which he does frequently in essays such as "Will Has Read Another Book," he is hardly working with an original theme.[16] Similarly, when he satirizes formal education, as he does in "The Secret of Education," because there is too much emphasis on "Political Science, International Relations, Drama, Buck Dancing, Sociology, Latin, Greek, [and] Art" and too little emphasis on reading, writing, and spelling, he is again virtually parroting the original Puritans' prejudice against any form of book learning that was not practical or teaching biblical lessons (206). The difference, of course, is that he was doing it for satirical and humorous effects. The Puritans were doing it to exercise intellectual and theological control over their parishioners and townspeople.

This bias against book learning is one of the oldest themes in American cultural history, one that quite literally came over on the Mayflower. Furthermore, this theme is guaranteed to find a sympathetic ear with virtually any American audience—film, radio, newspaper, or otherwise. This is not to deny Will Rogers's genius for comedy. But it does suggest that he had an equally keen intuitive sense of the cultural forces that determined how a typical American audience would be predisposed to react to any given subject matter—including book learning.[17]

In their own writings, most of the Puritans also favored a "plain style," one that avoided literary allusions and rhetorical embellishments and excesses. In essence, their writing style was similar to their manner of dress: simple, plain, and unadorned. They looked askance at anything that violated this plain style. For example, when Hester Prynne is standing on the scaffold in Nathaniel Hawthorne's *The Scarlet Letter* (1850), with the letter *A* on her chest, which she has embellished "with an elaborate embroidery and fantastic flourishes of gold thread," she is clearly rebelling against the plain style of dress favored by the Puritans.[18] But she is also the symbol of the artist (writer) who utilizes such "elaborate" and "fantastic flourishes" of rhetorical styles, all of which the Puritans distrusted. Indeed, they saw these pretentious artistic or literary devices as clever tricks that were used to deceive the reader, distort the truth, and conceal the writer's true intentions.

In part this celebration of the plain style, and the simultaneous rejection of a more rhetorically elaborate style, was due to the Puritans' faith in the King James Bible, especially the Book of Proverbs, which had been written in the plain style, and which the Puritans quoted extensively. They also believed the rest of world literature, much of which they considered to be written with these rhetorical excesses and embellishments, was an attempt to subvert the simple wisdom of scripture.[19] It could be argued that this plain style developed into the style favored by mainstream American humorists and satirists; whereas the more rhetorically elaborate style, which in the minds of the original Puritans was an extension of the British and European literary traditions, led to the failed traditions in American humor and satire.

The Puritans' belief that the best writing styles express simple wisdom in a plain style is eventually reflected in the aphorisms of William Bradford, John Winthrop, Ben Franklin, Mark Twain, and Will Rogers.[20] Note, for example, that although the subject matters are frequently different in the following list of aphorisms, there are stylistic similarities as the authors attempt to express simple wisdom in a plain style. Note also how the seriousness of the Puritan writers Bradford and Winthrop evolves gradually into the wit and cleverness of Ben Franklin. This, in turn, is then transformed into the humor and satire of Mark Twain and Will Rogers—even though the plain style, and much of the simple wisdom, remains relatively unchanged:

BOOK OF PROVERBS

> If thou faint in the day of adversity, thy struggle is small.
>
> A wise man is strong; yet a man of knowledge increases strength.
>
> He that gathereth in summer is a wise son: but he that sleepeth in harvest is a son that causeth shame.
>
> He becometh poor that dealeth with a slack hand; but the hand of the diligent maketh rich.

## WILLIAM BRADFORD (1590–1657), GOVERNOR OF PLYMOUTH PLANTATION

By which it appears how one wicked person may infect many, and what care all ought to have what servants they bring into their families.

Where the Lord begins to sow good seed, there the envious man will endeavour to sow tares.

For how unperfect and lame is the work of grace in that person who wants charity to cover a multitude of offenses.

## JOHN WINTHROP (1588–1649), GOVERNOR OF MASSACHUSETTS BAY

We account him a good servant, who breaks not his covenant.

When you agree with a workman to build you a ship or house, he undertakes as well for his skill as for his faithfulness, for it is his profession, and you pay him for both.

The law of nature could give no rules for dealing with enemies, for all are to be considered friends in the estate of innocency.

## BEN FRANKLIN (1706–1790)

To bear other peoples afflictions, everyone has courage and enough to spare.

Admiration is the daughter of ignorance.

In this world nothing is sure but death and taxes.

The sleeping fox catches no poultry.

The rotten apple spoils his companion.

MARK TWAIN (1835–1910)

> By trying we can learn to endure adversity—another man's I mean.
>
> The older we grow the greater becomes our wonder at how much ignorance we can contain without bursting one's clothes.
>
> What is the difference between a taxidermist and a tax collector? The taxidermist takes only your skin.

WILL ROGERS (1879–1935)

> Everything is funny, as long as it is happening to somebody else.
>
> Everyone is ignorant only on different subjects.
>
> We don't seem to be able to check crime, so why not legalize it and then tax it out of business.
>
> I am no fisherman, and hope I never get lazy enough to take it up.

Will Rogers roughens up the language to more closely approximate the American idiom and dialect spoken by common people, as did Ben Franklin and Mark Twain before him. Still, he is utilizing the plain style and expressing much of the same simple wisdom that the Puritans expressed or quoted from the Book of Proverbs, only he is using it for humorous effect.

The earliest Puritans also lived lives that were carefully programmed. There was little room for spontaneity. Everything—meals, church activities, even relaxation—was carefully scheduled. Spontaneity itself was viewed with great suspicion. It could be argued that this kind of programmed, overly mechanical lifestyle also created a deeply felt need to be more spontaneous. The rare moments when they could be more free and spontaneous must have been precious and revitalizing. This same work ethic, with very little in the way of relaxation, created a strong national economy. However, it also created a workforce with little time to just unwind and be something more than workers.

Will Rogers sensed some of the same yearnings in his stage audiences. Rather than acknowledge that some of what he did on stage was the result of hard work and rehearsals, he denied that careful planning or conscious craftsmanship had anything to do with his stage performances. Rather, in his essay "The Extemporaneous Line," he emphasizes the extemporaneous and spontaneous nature of much that he did on stage:

> Of late all I am asked is 'Who writes your stuff and where do you get it?' And the surprising answer is: The newspapers write it? All I do is to get all the papers I can carry and then read all that is going on and try to figure out the main things that the audience has just read, and talk on that . . . Lots of good subjects have been in the papers for days and I can't think of a thing on them. Some of the best things come to me when I am on the stage. I figure out the few subjects that I will touch on and always have a few gags on each one, but the thing I may go out to say may fall flat and some other gag I just happen to put in out there goes great . . . this illustrates my work. I have to have my idea—all extemporaneous speakers do—but my laugh comes quickly and apparently out of nowhere (3).

In one respect, Rogers is telling the truth here, at least to the extent that he clearly had a quick and inventive mind; and he was able to create much of his material spontaneously while he was actually on stage. But he is also being somewhat less than candid about the hours of preparation he put into his stage act, and later his radio shows. Peter Rollins writes that unpublished radio notes of shows Will Rogers did from 1927 to 1935 reveal that "Rogers studied for his presentations and that his extemporaneous manner was the product of an artist" (258).

Why did Will Rogers emphasize the extemporaneous nature of his stage act and radio shows, while at the same time not always revealing the careful craftsmanship and conscious artistry that went into his performances? One of the reasons is that his Oklahoma cowboy, like any effective stage or literary persona, needs this aura of spontaneity to be believable and entertaining. If it ever became clear to Will Rogers's audiences that some of the seemingly extemporaneous responses were in actuality contrived and/or prepared in advance, the Oklahoma cowboy persona would undoubtedly have lost a good deal of his innocence, charm, and perhaps even his credibility.

Will Rogers was not deliberately misleading his audiences. Given the stage personality of the Oklahoma cowboy with all of his apparent charm and innocence, he had no choice but to emphasize the spontaneity of whatever this persona said and did on stage. Conscious artistry and careful craftsmanship, as well as his ability to extemporize, were all necessary to create a stage and literary persona as convincing and as enduring as the Oklahoma cowboy.

Intuitive reader of the culture that he was, Will Rogers undoubtedly also sensed that American audiences were suspicious of the "artifice" of art and artists, and so he instinctively chose to completely conceal himself within his stage and literary persona. This way the artist ceases to exist. Not only was he now the Oklahoma cowboy, but this strategy also protected Will Rogers, the artist, from the biases of his culture. In the process, he demonstrated his ability to position both himself and his stage and literary persona on the side of American cultural values where they would have the greatest audience appeal. The other side of those cultural values, on which many American "artists" have found themselves, would have nowhere near the universal appeal of the working-class Oklahoma cowboy persona who appeared to be one and the same as his creator.

The original New England Puritans also tended to judge everything by whether or not it had a "high moral purpose." Their lives, social customs, political activities, and legal systems were molded around this sense that everything that involved the public had to have a solid moral center. The original New England Puritans were, thus, "moralists" in the most traditional and inflexible sense of the term. This is immediately evident in the writings of virtually all the early Puritan leaders, including William Bradford, John Winthrop, Thomas Hooker, John Cotton, Increase Mather, Cotton Mather, and others who settled in either Plymouth Plantation or Massachusetts Bay. Indeed, the original Puritans came to the New World to cleanse themselves and to strengthen their resolve so they could someday return to the Old World and restore its moral vision. Everything they did centered around their stated desires to strengthen their resolve and refine that moral vision.

In this context, we should note that Will Rogers, who arrived on the scene almost three hundred years later, was in many respects a Puritan at heart—as was Mark Twain before him. In spite of his humorous and satirical approaches to life, Will Rogers is at the core an old-fashioned moralist, not in the grimly serious and inflexible sense that we associate with the original Puritans. He had much too charitable a soul to fall into those traps. Will Rogers's moral sense, as expressed through humor, reminds us more of the tolerant and forgiving moral vision of Roger Williams, who founded Rhode Island to avoid the moral and religious excesses of the original Puritan communities, and William Penn, who founded Pennsylvania for the same reasons (Parrington, 62–75).

Unlike much American humor, there is a moral center to almost everything Will Rogers writes and everything he utters on stage, even though it might not be immediately apparent to his audiences. His satires on government and politics had a common theme: that these institutions, which were designed to respond to the needs of the people and to provide leadership, often lose their moral focus and, therefore, their ability to lead effectively. This is evident in his essays, including "Congress at Work," "Truth in Politics," "Raid the Treasury," "The Election Campaign," and "Congress Is Funniest When It's Serious." Similarly, essays and columns such as "Whooping It Up for Wall Street," "What the Farmer Needs," and "Who Runs the Stock Exchange" subtly, and sometimes not so subtly, chide big businesses for losing their moral center and becoming much too greedy and exploitative of the lower classes.

Will Rogers's attitude towards women, especially his squeamishness regarding anything to do with human sexuality, reflects another close attachment to the subterranean depths of a Puritan culture and sense of morality. When he writes about women in "What Women Need" and "The Wrong Impression of Women," he gently satirizes what he perceives to be feminine foibles and idiosyncrasies. He never addresses the issue of feminine sexuality in even the most mundane and least offensive manner.

In his personal life, Will Rogers also revealed himself to be a man whose decisions were often made within a moral framework that reflects his cultural antecedents. In his book *Our Will Rogers* (1953), Homer Croy writes:

> He rarely went to church and took no active interest in religious matters. But he never slurred religion and never took a superior attitude toward anyone who found solace in it. He wanted his children to have religious training and often, at the breakfast table on Sunday morning, would urge them to go to church. When the family was living in Beverly Hills, he found there was no church in the town; this disturbed him. However, he discovered a kind of Sunday School was being held each week in a grammar-school building. Will sent his own children and helped raise money to build a real church; the church still stands and is known today as the Beverly Hills Community Church (284).

Croy describes another event in Will Rogers's life that reveals the extent to which he made his life's decisions within a traditional moral framework, one that had an especially deep and profound respect for sexual morality. Croy points out that Will Rogers was required to kiss Irene Rich in one of his films, but he put the scene off as long as he could because he was uncomfortable with the idea of kissing someone other than his wife. Finally, the director pulled Irene Rich aside and told her to take control of the scene, since Will was obviously intimidated by the idea of a screen kiss. Later, after the scene had been completed, largely through Irene Rich's perseverance, Will exclaimed, "Good lord! I feel as if I'd been unfaithful to my wife" (266). Although this utterance might reflect Will's attempts to drift back into the security of his stage persona, his response seems genuine because observers reported that he was clearly distressed by this scene.

A similar event is described by Bryan and Frances Sterling in their book, *Will Rogers in Hollywood* (1984). According to these authors, when Will Rogers was appearing in a San Francisco production of Eugene O'Neill's play, *Ah, Wilderness!,* he received a letter from a clergyman chastising him for the "scene in which the father lectures the son on the subject of his relations with an immoral woman." According to the clergyman, that scene so embarrassed his young daughter that he took her by the hand, left the theater, and "has not been able to look her in the eye since." Bryan and Frances Sterling described Rogers's response to the letter:

> This so disturbed Rogers he finally withdrew from the play. He also asked to be released from his commitment to do the screen version for Metro-Goldwyn-Mayer, promising to do another film in its place as soon as a suitable script was found. While waiting, Will accepted an invitation from the famous pilot, Wiley Post, to fly around the world—the trip which ended in the death of both men (172).

Decisions of this type reveal a man whose moral values were grounded in a much earlier time in American history, a time that inevitably leads all the way back to the Puritans, but without the cruelty and enforced morality of a theocracy.

The Puritan obsession with the "work ethic" is another idea that is reflected in Will Rogers's life, career, and stage performances. The original Puritans celebrated individuals who worked with their hands, while they simultaneously abhorred idleness because they believed fervently that "Idle hands were the devil's playmates." The Puritans were, thus, partially responsible for establishing a culture that celebrated the callused hands of the working class, for they were the symbols of a virtuous lifestyle.[21]

Will Rogers is somewhat of a paradox. His involvements in radio, film and newspapers made him one of the busiest and most productive men in America. Yet, in his writings and public statements, he frequently implied that he hadn't done an honest day's work since he became an entertainer. In one respect he was telling the truth because he didn't think of entertainment as work. Nonetheless, through his slow drawl and laid-back, country manner, he clearly went out of his way to create the impression that he was somewhat of an idler—as did Mark Twain in the previous century. In part, Will Rogers did this because he was aware that his audiences themselves knew better. How could they not? Since he received more press coverage than virtually any other American in the early part of the twentieth century, certainly the American people were aware of his many interests and activities.

There were other reasons that suggest he not only adopted this stage demeanor to put his audience at ease, but also because he fully understood the meanings of the cultural symbols he was manipulating. His relationship to the Puritan, and later American, work ethic can be understood only if we carefully analyze his stage personality and demeanor in the context of the props he used in his act. In the Ziegfeld Follies, he appeared to be an idler, but he also created the impression that he was nothing more than a common working man (cowboy!) who was just taking a few minutes off to tell some yarns to the people gathered in the audience. During his monologue, he prominently displayed the symbols of this working-class status: his bandana scarf, worn boots, chaps, shirt-sleeves, battered cowboy hat, and especially his lasso, which he turned into a plaything to perform rope tricks for the enjoyment of his audience.

He turned symbols of work into symbols of play, which would be more acceptable in a Puritan culture. He was undoubtedly aware that he would not have been so readily accepted by his audiences if he had addressed them as an out-of-work idler. This would probably have violated the sensitivities of working-class men and women in a nation that celebrated the work ethic. However, as a working-class cowboy, who was surrounded by the tools of his trade and who had earned the right to relax for a few moments by doing rope tricks before returning to his labors, he struck a sympathetic chord with his audiences. They, too, were probably mostly working-class people who had earned a few hours of relaxation before returning to their jobs.

Through the film persona of "Jubilo," Will Rogers did create a "rural clown, a perpetual loafer who floats through society getting himself into trouble and avoiding work whenever possible" (Rollins, 54). But this character, although he did have a certain kind of charm, never achieved the permanent audience appeal of the working-class Oklahoma cowboy. Nor did Rogers ever seriously try to resurrect Jubilo after his film career and transform this persona into a permanent part of his repertoire. He probably understood that such a character functioned so far outside the mainstream of American culture, and was so alien to the work ethic, as to ultimately have limited audience appeal.

Throughout Rogers's career, one senses not only the mind of a clever artist, but also someone who instinctively understood cultural symbols and how to manipulate them to maximize the dramatic effect on his audiences. The sources of many of these cultural symbols are to be found in the seemingly distant Puritan colonies that took root in the New World almost three hundred years before Will Rogers ever set foot on a stage. He intuitively understood them, rejected many of their ideas, and utilized others to reach his audiences in ways very few performers before or after him managed to do.

Will Rogers read the culture about as well as it could be read. He didn't have to know anything about the original Puritans. Their ideas became American culture. Once he had instinctively read the values of that culture, which he did remarkably well, his intuition would tell him what would make them laugh.

It took a while, but someday we would also learn how to laugh at ourselves.

---

1. Walter Blair and Hamlin Hill, *America's Humor* (New York: Oxford University Press, 1978) 522.
2. Ketchum, 393.
3. Ketchum, 393.
4. Constance Rourke, *America Humor* (New York: Doubleday & Company Inc., 1931) 19–20.
5. Reverend H. R. Haweis, "From American Humorists (1882)," in *Critical Essays on American Humor*, eds. William Bedford Clark and W. Craig Turner (Boston: G. K. Hall & Co., 1984) 30.
6. Andrew Lang, "From 'American Humor' (1889), Critical Essays on American Humor, eds. William Bedford Clark and W. Craig Turner (Boston: G. K. Hall & Co., 1984) 31.
7. The pattern in which laughter is associated with sin and evil is apparent throughout Hawthorne's writings, including his classic novel *The Scarlet Letter* (1852). Many of the characters in the story reflect the Puritans' propensity to associate laughter with immoral activities. Hester Prynne's illegitimate daughter Pearl "laughed aloud" and shows no respect for the dead while she dances on the graves of her Puritan ancestors. Reverend Dimmesdale bursts into a "great peal of laughter" as he stands on the scaffold at night and watches other townspeople pass by in the darkness to engage in immoral activities. The captain and sailors of "the questionable vessel," who are probably pirates, engage in "laughter" and frivolous behavior at the end of the novel. The father of the Custom House is described as "an animal . . . with no heart, no soul, no mind . . . [nothing but a] laugh which perpetually reechoed through The Custom House."

8. Thomas Morton, "From New England Canaan (1632)," in *The Literature of America: Colonial Period*, ed. Larzer Ziff (New York: McGraw-Hill Book Company, 1970) 108.
9. Vernon Louis Parrington, *Main Currents in American Thought*, Vol. I (New York: Harcourt, Brace & World, Inc., 1927) 3–10.
10. All references in this paper to the poems of Anne Bradstreet and Edward Taylor are to their selected works in *Major American Poets*, ed. Francis Murphy (Lexington, Massachusetts: D. C. Heath and Company, 1967).
11. The Will Rogers Library contains almost a complete set of the tragedies and comedies of William Shakespeare. There is, however, no evidence that Will Rogers himself read these, or any other editions of Shakespeare's works.
12. Mark Twain, "How to Tell a Story," *The Norton Anthology of American Literature*, vol. 2, third edition (New York: W. W. Norton and Company, 1989) 216.
13. William Bradford, "From *History of Plymouth Plantation* (1620–1947)," in *The Literature of America: Colonial Period*, ed. Larzer Ziff (New York: McGraw-Hill Book Company, 1970) 81.
14. Janice Stout, *The Journey Narrative in American Literature* (Greenwood Press, 1983) ix.
15. Richard Hofstadter, *Anti-intellectualism in American Life* (New York: Alfred A. Knopf, 1970) 57–58.
16. Will Rogers, "Will Has Read Another Book," *A Will Rogers Treasury*, eds. Bryan B. and Frances N. Sterling (New York: Bonanza Books, 1982) 144.
17. The fact that Will Rogers used books more than he was willing to reveal to the general public is obvious through even a cursory examination of his personal library. It is true that he may not have read all of these books from cover to cover. However, he clearly used many of them as reference tools (especially the extensive collection of books on humor), for many of the bindings are worn and numerous pages are underlined. Will Rogers also had in his personal library an impressive collection of dictionaries and other similar reference books, including *Webster's New International Dictionary, Funk and Wagnall's Practical Standard Dictionary, Allen's Synonyms and Antonyms, 18,000 Words Often Mispronounced, Collins Home Dictionary, The Little Oxford Dictionary of Current English, The World Almanac and Book of Facts*, and other such books. Several of these reference books show signs of wear and extensive use. Since the children had a room for their own personal library and would probably at their age have not been interested in the above books anyhow, it seems clear that Will Rogers, in spite of his protestations to the contrary, may have been somewhat of a "closet reader."
18. Nathaniel Hawthorne, *The Scarlet Letter* (New York: New American Library, 1959) 60.
19. Hofstadter, 57–58.
20. The connections between Will Rogers, Ben Franklin, and Mark Twain will be dealt with in greater detail later in this book. For now, suffice it to say that Franklin and especially Twain were well represented in Will Rogers's personal library. Furthermore, some of their books appear to have been acquired by Will Rogers himself, rather than having been sent to him by his many fans and admirers. Similarly, Betty

Rogers apparently purchased all twenty-three volumes of the complete works of *Mark Twain*. Although there is little evidence that Will Rogers devoted much of his time to the works of these two American literary giants, the presence of their works in his library suggests that he was certainly aware of what Mark Twain and Ben Franklin represented to the development of American Literature and culture.

21. See Nathaniel Hawthorne's discussion of the dilemma of the American artist in a Puritan society in "The Custom House" introduction to *The Scarlet Letter*. Also see Nathaniel Hawthorne's short story, "The Artist of the Beautiful," for one of American literature's most insightful statements about a Puritan culture's attitude toward the work ethic. Robert Danforth, the symbol of the Puritan work ethic in this story, is held in high esteem by the community; whereas Owen Warland, the artist, is treated with disdain because he is not a man who does respectable work. In this context, Will Rogers in his Oklahoma cowboy persona is concealing the artist behind the far more respectable stage personality of the working-class cowboy.

# IV.

# BEN FRANKLIN AND THE COLONIAL WITS

THE PURITANS remained the dominant cultural force in the colonies from the time they first arrived in the early 1600s until well into the centuries that followed. No one was immune to their influence. Their ideas remained long after they were gone. Europeans, who viewed the gradual transformation of the colonies into a country, were probably more aware of their continued influence than people actually living in what would become the United States of America. Occasionally, when some seemingly new political or cultural upheaval would occur in America, it would be followed by comments from Europeans like, "There go those Puritans again."

By the mid- and late-1700s, the original Puritan settlers were long gone. Their descendants had mellowed, and in some ways even rejected the ideas of their theocratic ancestors. Executions of witches were no longer fashionable. There were other ways the original witch-hunt mentality manifested itself in America's evolving history. But, for the most part, the days of townspeople gathered around a scaffold to curse the accused witches and cheer when their bodies were hanging limp at the end of a rope—those days had ended.

Or had they?

It would take time for the "heathen wilderness" the original Puritans envisioned in the New World to be transformed by later generations into the "earthly paradise" somewhere on the western horizon. The humor of the eighteenth century was instrumental in assisting a departure from the Puritan's more radical theocratic impulses. The Puritans were slowly slipping into the substratum of our culture, but they would emerge again and again throughout our history. It was often the evolving humor that would help put their extreme ideas back into a more controllable place in our national consciousness.

From the founding of Plymouth Plantation in 1620 and Massachusetts Bay in 1628, until the opening of the frontier with the Louisiana Purchase in 1803, the best writing in the colonies did not flow from the pens of the satirists or humorists. As Walter Blair and Hamlin Hill point out in their book *Native American Humor (1800–1900),* there was a dearth of talented satirists and humorists in America until somewhat later in our nation's history:

> Though the colonists were more prolific of humor than is generally supposed, the beginnings of this type of writing [humorous writing] came late. And they were long coming because most American authors failed for a long time to perceive the richest comedy about them or to discover a technique which revealed that comedy (3–4).

The best writing in early Colonial America came instead from the pens of Thomas Jefferson, John Adams, Thomas Paine and others who helped frame the Declaration of Independence (1776), the Constitution (1787), and the various pamphlets and documents that were written to plot the early political destiny of this country. Nonetheless, even these serious essayists and pamphleteers contributed greatly to the future development of American satire and humor, primarily because they established the importance of literary personae in their respective writings. As Larzer Ziff points out in his anthology, *The Literature of America: Colonial Period* (1970), these men, and many others like them, were schooled "In the tradition of classical rhetoric which taught that not only was the subject matter shaped by the assumed nature of the audience, but the author buried his own personality in that of a penman whose assumed character provided the best voice for comment on the subject matter to that audience" (391).

In the 1780s, James Madison, Alexander Hamilton, and John Jay wrote a series of newspaper articles, which later became known as *The Federalist Papers* (1787–1788), that argued for the adoption of the Constitution. In this series, "Federalist Number 10" was supposedly written, not by the authors themselves, but rather by a writer who was identified only as "Publius," a representative voice speaking for the American public (Parrington, 288–292). Similarly, Thomas Paine wrote his famous political pamphlet "Common Sense" (1776) not so much from his own perspective, but rather from the perspective of common people speaking with the logic of common sense (334–343). And John Adams's "A Dissertation on the Canon and Feudal Law" (1765) first appeared anonymously "with the relevant facts about [the] author . . . revealed by a voice not a signature" (Ziff, 391).

Although these men were writing serious political, social, and economic treatises, they nonetheless introduced the idea of literary personae into American letters in the second half of the eighteenth century. Later, this became the single most important rhetorical skill utilized by the nineteenth- and twentieth-century satirists and humorists. In time, it could be argued, we almost became a nation of satirists and humorists who concealed their real identities behind pen names or literary personae.

There was a flurry of humorous and satirical writing in the American colonies shortly before, during, and after the Declaration of Independence and American Revolution in 1776. As Walter Blair and Hamlin Hill wrote in their book, *American's Humor from Poor Richard to Doonesbury* (1978), "in the late eighteenth and early nineteenth centuries, when New England was no longer a Puritan stronghold, respectable colonial humor exerted influence. The Revolutionary War triggered political satire to redress wrongdoing of a social rather than a religious nature."[1]

By this time in our nation's history, England was firmly entrenched as the symbol of established power and cultural elitism in the New World. The colonies were cast in the role of the commoners. They were the disadvantaged and persecuted outsiders rebelling against a world controlled by a privileged upper class. Conditions were ripe for the satirists and humorists who had been suppressed in a Puritan culture to assert themselves—and they did. It could be argued that the seeds of American humor and satire were sown with the decision of the original Puritans to flee to the New World, thus placing them outside of the European establishment. However, the germination process did not begin in earnest until several years before open hostilities between England and the colonies were about to commence.

The satire written during the colonial period tended to reflect one of two very different literary traditions. It was either an extension of the seventeenth- and eighteenth-century British satirical tradition of John Dryden and Alexander Pope, which was distinguished primarily by its intellectual style and tone. This satirical tradition, as it was practiced in the colonies, ultimately became the failed humorous tradition in America. For an American audience, the *manner* of telling the story was more important than the *matter* of telling the story. This was a crucial distinction, and one Mark Twain articulated later in his essay, "How to Tell a Story" (216). This satirical tradition, which can be traced directly from Ben Franklin to Mark Twain to Will Rogers, recognized the importance of the *manner* of telling the story, usually with idiomatic expressions and slang, and it eventually became mainstream American satire and humor.[2]

The writers known as the Hartford Wits are examples of the British tradition, and Ben Franklin (1706–1790) is an example of the evolving American literary tradition. The Hartford Wits—which included writers such as Joel Barlow (1754–1812), John Trumbull (1751–1831), Timothy Dwight (1752–1817), and others—were somewhat of a paradox. At the same time that they sought to celebrate the American experience, primarily through their attempts to write epic poems about our nation's early experiences in the New World, they often only succeeded in perpetuating a poor imitation of the European literary traditions, especially its satirical and humorous traditions. In the process, the Hartford Wits failed to develop literary forms that could serve as models for future American writers. They were, instead, committed to a literary tradition that was incompatible with the uniqueness of the American experience and subject matters. Perhaps the former colonies simply needed more time to become accustomed to their new status as a country before more authentic American artistic and literary forms could evolve.

The Hartford Wits did not provide a bridge between the original New England Puritans and the nineteenth- and twentieth-century American humorists. That bridge is provided by Ben Franklin, an authentic American genius who clearly evolved out of the Puritan past. Although he had been influenced by the British writers Joseph Addison and Richard Steele, he was instrumental in developing the native tradition in American humor and satire and propelling it into the next two centuries. In the process, his ideas were absorbed into the culture and inevitably passed on, in one form or another, to each successive generation of American writers.

Although some American writers, including Mark Twain, outwardly rejected his ideas, Ben Franklin provided this nation with literary devices that were far more compatible with American stories and subject matters. He became a literary father to our country, including Will Rogers whose life and career parallels Franklin's in some truly remarkable ways. The importance of Ben Franklin is that he not only reshaped this nation's political destiny, but also its culture. Will Rogers at a later date, attuned as he was to the deepest wellsprings of American culture, inherited these ideas from Ben Franklin as certainly as if he had received a lengthy letter in the mail from this eighteenth-century genius. If one believes in reincarnation, one would almost have to conclude that Ben Franklin was reincarnated late in the nineteenth century as Will Rogers.[3]

To understand the connections between Ben Franklin and Will Rogers, it is important to first understand the significance of the Hartford Wits, whose work constituted the failed tradition in American humor and satire. These early satirists, who perpetuated the British satirical tradition, illuminate by contrast the more authentic American satirical tradition of which Will Rogers is an extension.

The Hartford Wits were a group of professional men, mostly Yale graduates, who met shortly after the Revolutionary War until the end of the century to discuss literature and politics, and to write poetry. Politically, they were Federalists, members of the party of Alexander Hamilton, which was sympathetic to the colonial upper class and wealthy business elite. They were less sympathetic to the Anti-Federalists or Jeffersonians, the political party that was more concerned with the needs of common working-class men and women. One of the stated literary goals of the Hartford Wits was to write an epic poem that would celebrate the American experience. They wanted a poem that would do for America what Virgil had done for ancient Rome with his masterpiece the *Aeneid* (17–19 BCE), and what Homer had done for ancient Greece with his epic poems the *Iliad* (ninth century BCE) and the *Odyssey* (ninth century BCE).

Timothy Dwight, one of the Hartford Wits and also the president of Yale University, wrote the first of these tedious American epics, which was published under the title *The Conquest of Canaan* (1785). Joel Barlow, another of the Hartford Wits, contributed an early version of his epic poem *The Vision of Columbus*, which was later to be entitled *The Columbiad* (1807). Published at great expense and amidst much fanfare, *The Columbiad* was at first celebrated as a major literary accomplishment, but its lofty, pretentious tone, creaky epic machinery, and tedious rhyming couplets were eventually rejected by readers.[4]

The opening stanza of the epic poem illustrates why future readers were not enthusiastic about Barlow's early attempt to celebrate the emerging New World in the West:

> I sing the Mariner who first unfurl'd
> An eastern banner o'er the western world,
> And taught mankind where future empires lay
> In these fair confines of descending day;
> Who sway'd a moment, with vicarious power,
> Iberia's scepter on the new found shore,
> Then saw the paths his virtuous steps had trod,
> Pursued by avarice and defined with blood,
> The tribes he foster'd with paternal toil
> Snatch'd from his hand, and slaughter'd for their spoil.[5]

One can almost hear Will Rogers reading these opening lines of *The Columbiad* and condensing them into a few short words: "Yup, we sure taught those European folks how to build a better country."

The Hartford Wits also wrote satire, of which John Trumbull's poem "The Progress of Dullness" (1793) and Joel Barlow's poem "The Hasty Pudding" (1793) are two representative examples. Trumbull's poem, a satire written in rhyming couplets and monotonous iambic tetrameter, satirized the Yale University curriculum, while Barlow's poem is a mock-epic that celebrates the virtues of American values and country life. Both poems are considered today to be, if not failures, at least works of limited literary value. In *Native American Humor* (1800–1890), Walter Blair writes of "The Hasty Pudding" that it "deals with a scene of the sort a nineteenth century humorist would be delighted to treat . . . But a typical American humorist, writing in the style of the [nineteenth] century which produced American humor, would be pretty sure to use even more details than does this unusually detailed eighteenth century description . . . the later humorists would [also] be pretty sure to record much conversation, catching the dialect, the intonations, the characteristics which revealed themselves in speech" (16).

Although Blair believes Barlow's poem, "The Hasty Pudding," is perhaps the best example of eighteenth-century American poetic satire, he also recognizes that it is only moderately effective because it fails to capture the American idiom and dialects. Blair argues the other poems written by the eighteenth-century American satirists are virtually all failures because the authors had not yet developed a "perception of the comic possibilities of the American scene and American character, [nor had they developed] a fictional technique which would reveal them" (16).

There are other reasons why most of these eighteenth-century attempts at humor and satire did not take hold in the colonies. These reasons enable us to understand the more successful tradition of American humor that leads inevitably to Mark Twain in the nineteenth and Will Rogers in the twentieth century:

- The Hartford Wits were following in the English literary tradition and not what would become the evolving American literary tradition. Hence, their classic epic machinery and tedious rhyming couplets did not resonate with newly formed audiences. This literary tradition in America would gradually fade in importance, whereas the evolving native tradition would lead to Walt Whitman's (1819–1892) epic poem *Leaves of Grass,* which he wrote and rewrote over many years. He wanted to create the impression of a poem as an organic, living entity that was a much better fit for the sprawling, diverse nation that was forming throughout the nineteenth century.

- The Hartford Wits' choice of tedious rhyming couplets and stilted iambic pentameter meters made their poems even more pretentious and tedious to read, as opposed to Whitman's poems which were written in unrhymed free verse.

- The Hartford Wits' choice of the pompous, almost godlike epic voice, when used to describe unpretentious people, places, and events, created an untenable point of view for American audiences.
- The Hartford Wits' decision to elevate the intelligence and awareness of the point of view did not reflect the propensities of an evolving nation without a sophisticated cultural or historical past.
- The Hartford Wits did not significantly deviate from Standard English and grammatically correct precision in sentence structure which, when used to describe poorly educated or semiliterate or illiterate people, undermined their attempts at satire and humor.
- The Hartford Wits presented themselves as members of a cultural elite addressing a less privileged audience, whereas the more successful tradition in American humor almost always reversed those roles.
- The Hartford Wits presented themselves as members of a political party that was sympathetic to an upper class, wealthy elite, whereas mainstream American humorists usually identify with the political concerns of common people.
- The Hartford Wits, most of whom were Yale University graduates, were part of the academic tradition in American humor and satire, whereas mainstream American humor usually evolved out of a grassroots popular culture that is often in opposition to the academic tradition.
- The Hartford Wits also found themselves on the side of "book learning," which for an American humorist like Will Rogers, who came on the scene much later, was strategically indefensible.
- The Hartford Wits were too verbose, whereas the more successful American humorists evolved out of the plain style that tended to prefer brevity over verbosity.

- The Hartford Wits tended to use artistically pretentious versions of themselves as their speakers, whereas more successful American humorists use lower-class, uneducated speakers to appeal to a much broader base of readers and audiences.

If we place Will Rogers in the context of each of the above issues, it becomes clear that he is not in any way an extension of this humorous and satirical tradition in American humor and storytelling. He was much too artistically intuitive to place himself, as did the Hartford Wits, in such a strategically indefensible position with respect to American cultural values and audiences.

With respect to each of these issues, we can say of Will Rogers:

- He was outside the European satirical tradition and very much in touch with his native humorous and satirical traditions.
- He avoided virtually all of the established literary genres, preferring instead simple, down-home storytelling and other rural American prose forms.
- Rather than adopt the epic voice, or any other established literary voice, he chose instead to adopt the far more modest, unpretentious, self-effacing voice of the Oklahoma cowboy persona.
- On the surface, he downgraded the intelligence of the Oklahoma cowboy persona, while subtly providing him with an abundance of common sense and simple wisdom.[6]
- He roughed up the language to imitate idiomatic expressions that reflected vernacular speech patterns of the type that would be used by average, everyday Americans.
- Far from presenting himself as a member of a cultural elite, he used the persona of the Oklahoma cowboy, a member of the working class, to gently satirize the pretentiousness of privileged classes and groups of people.

- He was shrewd enough to avoid any political entanglements or alienating the wealthy and powerful elite, while making it clear that both he and his Oklahoma cowboy persona were advocates for common, everyday Americans.[7]

- Even though he was better educated than the average American of his time, he created the impression that he had little formal schooling, thus placing himself even further outside of the academic tradition—which he then satirized.

- Similarly, he positioned himself on the side of the American people and their attitudes toward "book learning," which the Oklahoma cowboy made clear, with the ropes and tools that surrounded him on stage, was inferior to experience.[8]

- He understood the relationship between brevity and effective satire, and he proclaimed proudly in his essay "The Extemporaneous Line," that he always did "the shortest act of any monologue man" (4).

- He developed a stage and literary persona that was a reflection of himself, perhaps even the dominant side of his personality; but rather than make this persona more pretentious, he transformed it instead into a modest, self-effacing, gum-chewing cowboy.

If we are to search for the early sources of Will Rogers's humor, we will not find them in the traditions established by the Hartford Wits and other groups of humorists who emerged during the colonial period in American history. We must turn instead to Ben Franklin, who qualifies as nothing less than Will Rogers's literary and philosophical mentor. It would be impossible to live in America without encountering Ben Franklin and his influence on American culture. And Will Rogers was very sensitive, both consciously and intuitively, to the forces that shaped American culture—especially humorous storytelling traditions.

Franklin's presence in American culture can be felt everywhere. It can even be felt in novels that appeared much later in our history. In F. Scott Fitzgerald's *The Great Gatsby* (1925), young Jay Gatsby wrote his personal rules for success on the inside back cover of a Hopalong Cassidy comic book. These rules included: "Study electricity"; "Practice elocution, poise and how to attain it"; "Study needed inventions"; and "Read one improving book or magazine per week." These rules, which are all listed under a carefully prepared daily "SCHEDULE," come directly from Ben Franklin's writings in his *Autobiography* (1771–1790), *Poor Richard's Almanac* (1733 - 1746), and/or "The Way to Wealth" (1758).[9]

The fact that Jay Gatsby's (Ben Franklin's) rules for success were listed in a western comic book demonstrates how Fitzgerald understood that Hopalong Cassidy and the other heroes of western comic books were extensions of Franklin's favorite persona of the noble American rustic. It also revealed Fitzgerald's understanding that American *popular culture*, even more than *high culture*, had perpetuated the teachings of Ben Franklin and passed them along from one generation to the next.

We could substitute "Will Rogers" for "F. Scott Fitzgerald," the "Oklahoma cowboy" for "Jay Gatsby," and "western novels"—which Will loved to read—for "western comic books," and the same general points would still be valid. The heroes of many of these western novels were latter-day versions of Ben Franklin's favorite persona of the "noble rustic."[10] Whether or not Jay Gatsby read any of Franklin's books or essays is unknown. The fact that he is so clearly parroting Franklin in his own personal rules for success means that both Jay Gatsby and F. Scott Fitzgerald obviously at some point encountered the ideas of this eighteenth-century genius.

The same can be said for Will Rogers. Even though he had a copy of Ben Franklin's *Poor Richard's Almanack* in his library, whether he read any of Franklin's works is ultimately insignificant.[11] He may not even have understood the extent to which he and his Oklahoma cowboy persona were indebted to Ben Franklin. Will Rogers instinctively took many of the ideas that Franklin had reshaped out of a Puritan culture, and he used the newly emerging electronic media to promote those ideas and his Oklahoma cowboy persona among the largest national audience ever assembled in America at the time.

In many respects, the lives and careers of Ben Franklin and Will Rogers, although they are separated by almost two centuries, have remarkable similarities:

- Even though Ben Franklin had the support of his newspaperman brother, he became the national symbol of a self-made man who, through sheer will-power and perseverance, rose from rags to riches (Ziff, 583–584); Will Rogers, even though his influential family helped pave the way to his success, similarly became the national symbol of a twentieth-century self-made man (Rollins, 3–4).
- Franklin is generally credited with having discovered the basic principles of electricity; Rogers, probably more than any of his contemporaries, learned how to use the electronic media to promote his Oklahoma cowboy persona among a national film and radio audience (Rollins, 6).
- Franklin was one of the most powerful men of his time, more powerful even than many presidents; Rogers was also one of the most powerful men of his time—so influential that some people urged him to run for the presidency, while others considered the presidency to be a step down for him.
- Franklin was considered by many in Europe and others at home to be the living embodiment of the American spirit; Rogers was considered by his own countrymen and others overseas to be the very epitome of the American character.
- Franklin, among many of his countrymen, achieved the status of a cultural icon in his own lifetime; Rogers achieved a similar status, as was evident by the outpouring of public grief at his untimely death, which affected the American people as much as the death of Abraham Lincoln had affected them seventy years earlier (Croy, 388).
- Franklin became an international ambassador who negotiated treaties and represented American interests in Europe; Rogers was an unofficial American ambassador throughout much of the world later in his life.
- Franklin, for many years, wrote satirical newspaper articles for his brother's newspaper; Rogers, during the last fifteen years of

his life, wrote a satirical column that appeared in many of the nation's newspapers.

- Franklin understood the anti-intellectual bias of his American audience, and he played it for all it was worth with "characters such as Silence Dogood, Poor Richard, Father Abraham, and old Daddy Ben" (Blair and Hill, 71); Rogers understood this same anti-intellectual bias with his Oklahoma cowboy persona, and he too played it for all it was worth with statements such as "there is nothing as stupid as an educated man if you get him off the thing he was educated in" (Ketchum, 401).
- Franklin's aphorisms, which are filled with common sense and simple wisdom, have been so thoroughly integrated into American culture as to be regarded by many today as platitudes and clichés; Rogers's aphorisms, which are similarly filled with common sense and simple wisdom, are still widely quoted.
- Franklin, when he was an American ambassador in Europe, played the role of noble American rustic to the hilt when he dressed in plain clothes, wore a frontiersman's fur cap instead of a powdered wig, and carried a walking stick crafted out of a young sapling.[12] Rogers, throughout his life, tried to convince the public that he and his equally rustic Oklahoma cowboy persona were also one and the same.
- Franklin, even though he consorted with some of the wealthiest and most influential people of his time, always considered himself an advocate for common people and their causes;[13] Rogers, even though he frequently moved in social circles that involved many of the most wealthy and influential people of his time, remained a lifelong member of the Democratic Party, which he felt was more sympathetic to the plight of the common people. However, he was mostly apolitical and refused to align himself with either party.

There were also some striking differences between Ben Franklin and Will Rogers:

- Franklin, probably because of his more intimate involvement with the political process on the national level, made many enemies. John Adams called him "an idler, a diplomatic ignoramus, a hypocrite, a wheeler-dealer, a publicity hound, a lecher, a sybarite, and an embezzler" (Blair and Hill, 54); Rogers had very few enemies on the national stage (Croy, ix).
- Franklin's aphorisms reflect the importance of getting ahead in life and even becoming wealthy, although perhaps not in the stereotypical way Mark Twain portrayed him to be (Blair and Hill, 55). Rogers never spoke of the accumulation of wealth as being that important to him. It also ran counter to his persona of the working-class Oklahoma cowboy who was content with his status in life.
- Franklin, especially in his political satires directed against British tyranny, could be devastatingly satirical; Rogers, who might have written similar satire had he lived long enough to see what Adolf Hitler did to Europe in World War II, seldom demeaned or destroyed the victims of his satire.[14]
- Franklin lived a long life and died of natural causes at the age of eighty-four; Rogers died at the relatively young age of fifty-five, one of our first celebrities to be killed in a plane crash.

Still, when we analyze the accomplishments of the two men—especially their literary accomplishments—we are once again forced to recognize an overwhelming number of similarities. Even though Franklin would occasionally experiment with satirical verse, he, like Will Rogers, normally preferred simple prose forms that captured vernacular speech patterns and idiomatic expressions. In the process, he discovered the distinction between American, British, and French satire that Mark Twain would eventually articulate in the next century in his essay, "How to Tell a Story." According to Twain, "The humorous story is American, the comic story is English, the witty story is French. The humorous story depends for its effect upon the *manner* of the telling; the comic story and the witty story upon the matter" (216).

Although Twain never acknowledged any indebtedness to Ben Franklin—in fact, he considered Franklin's simple aphorisms and homespun philosophies to be abhorrent—in retrospect, it seems clear that Twain, and indeed every subsequent American humorist or satirist, was greatly indebted to Franklin. Without Franklin's experiments with vernacular speech patterns and idiomatic expressions, it seems highly doubtful that American humor and satire would have come of age in the nineteenth century (Blair and Hill, 53–54).

Ben Franklin also developed almost a hundred masks and literary personae in his writings (Blair and Hill, 75). Most of these were variations of the one persona he apparently preferred over all others: the noble American rustic, a character who would dominate American humor and literature in the nineteenth century. Ernest Hemingway credits Mark Twain with this discovery when he said, "all modern American literature comes from one book by Mark Twain called *Adventures of Huckleberry Finn*."[15] However, there probably wouldn't have been a Huckleberry Finn if Ben Franklin hadn't established literary models and devices that led inevitably to Twain's development of this iconic character. If Mark Twain hadn't developed this persona by using vernacular speech patterns and idiomatic expressions, it is also conceivable that we might never have known Will Rogers and his Oklahoma cowboy persona.

At the very least, it seems clear that neither Mark Twain nor Will Rogers would have succeeded to the extent that they did in their respective stage and literary careers had not Ben Franklin's early experiments with literary personae shown American writers an alternative to the British satirical tradition.

Nowhere is this more apparent than in Franklin's feminine persona, Silence Dogood. Some of the satire is in the name choice itself. This persona is quite opinionated and seldom "silent" about anything. In "Silence Dogood No. 4," she ponders the question of whether her young son William should pursue a "college education." She hopes, however, that he "will take his learning very well, and not idle away his time as many there now-a-days do."

Later, she falls asleep and has a dream that she is traveling through a "pleasant and delightful field . . . to a Famous Temple of Learning." Along the way, she realizes that every peasant is "preparing to send one of his children to the famous place . . . [even though] those who were travelling thither were little better than Dunces and Blockheads." She becomes increasingly aware that those same children will "learn little more than how to carry themselves handsomely, and enter a Room genteely." Silence concludes that once they graduate from the Temple of Learning they will be "as great Blockheads as ever, only more proud and self-centered." Only in the last two sentences do we learn that the Temple of Learning where these "Blockheads" become even "more proud and self-centered" is Harvard University.[16]

In this short sketch and other Silence Dogood stories, we see clear evidence of the dominant emerging American literary persona. Silence Dogood, the lower-class rural literary persona, unloads an anti-intellectual, albeit hilarious critique of colleges and college-educated students of her time. That Franklin would even think of creating a feminine voice to deliver this message is truly remarkable. The American feminine voice itself would not be shaped and refined for many years to come.

The Silence Dogood persona is a great leap forward in the evolution of American humor. She is the voice of rural America, tweaking the nose of the political, business, and educational elite in the colonies. Ben Franklin's major contributions to American humor and satire involve his experiments with vernacular speech patterns, idiomatic expressions, and various forms of literary personae. In almost every case, Franklin shaped the literary persona of the "noble rustic" that will dominate the American stage into the nineteenth and twentieth centuries.

Will Rogers's Oklahoma cowboy persona is, in many respects, another "noble rustic" of the type Ben Franklin created during the colonial period in American history. The Oklahoma cowboy is "rustic" to the extent that he wears leather chaps and boots, which connect him to nature; and his broad, wide-eyed smile and seemingly naïve, innocent demeanor silently communicate the subliminal message to his audiences that "this is a young man from the country." Still, the Oklahoma cowboy is "noble" to the extent that he openly displays his rope and other symbols of this working-class status; and he speaks in a plain language that is filled with wisdom and common sense.

The major difference, as one would expect from two writers separated by almost a full century, is the language and word choices. Franklin, although he often poses as the noble rustic, is still writing for the most part in the English language we inherited from Great Britain. Some of the word choices in Silence Dogood's monologues are slightly modified, proper English phrases that reflect Franklin's own education. In his autobiography, he proudly describes his educational accomplishments and attitudes toward book learning: "My early Readiness in Learning to read (which must have been very early, as I do not remember when I could not read) and the Opinion of all [my father's] Friends that I should certainly make a good scholar." Then he adds, again with considerable pride, "I had risen gradually from the Middle of the Class of that Year to be Head of it, and farther was mov'd into the next class above it, in order to go with the third at the end of the year" (273).

Will Rogers addresses the same issues of book learning and education in one of his "Will Rogers Says" newspaper columns: "Well, all I know is just what I read in the papers and what little I get from just the names and taking little glances in books. You know I am the 'durndest' fellow. People send me more books. Now I am 52 years old, sound of body, but weak of mind, and I never did read hardly any books. Oh, every once in a while I will hear 'em blabbing about one so much till I try to take some time off and read one."[17]

Will Rogers reflects the nineteenth-century generation of American humorists who made the complete break with the English language we inherited. He replaced it with an ungrammatical form of American English and speakers of lower intelligence and limited education, but filled with common sense. In many ways, the Oklahoma cowboy is a more humorous, less formally educated, but nonetheless wise and insightful version of Ben Franklin and some of the noble rustic personae he created a century earlier.[18]

---

1. Walter Blair and Hamlin Hill, *America's Humor from Poor Richard to Doonesbury.* (New York: Oxford University Press, 1978) 174.
2. Although there is little in Will Rogers's personal library to suggest that he read or was familiar with the colonial satirists and humorists, he was certainly familiar with their twentieth-century descendants. The largest single category in Will Rogers's

personal library is the section devoted to his collections of books of jokes, humorous stories, cartoons, and other such materials. These books have numerous pages that are marked and/or underlined, thus suggesting that they may have been used for his monologues and/or newspaper articles. These books were written by various American humorists, including James Thurber, Groucho Marx, Ogden Nash, Irvin Cobb, and other such writers and comedians. Other books written by humorists such as Harry Lauder and Mr. Dooley, whose plain styles and satirical appeals to common sense are somewhat reminiscent of both the colonial satirists and of Will Rogers's own humorous style, are similarly underlined and marked up. Once again, these well-used books seem to indicate that Will Rogers, a man who satirized "book learning" in many of his monologues and newspaper articles, nonetheless frequently used books as convenient "reference tools." These books may also suggest that Will Rogers *was* adopting the persona of the Oklahoma cowboy when he made statements such as, "Well, all I know is just what I read in the papers," since Rogers clearly knew many things that he read elsewhere—including the information he apparently gathered from the humorous books in his personal library.

3. Will Rogers's personal library contains one book on Ben Franklin, which was written by Phillips Russell and titled *Benjamin Franklin, The First Civilized American.* A memorandum (2/16/70) written by Edward A. Earl, area manager of the Will Rogers State Park in the California State Department of Parks and Recreation, cites fifty-nine (59) volumes that were missing from the 1970 inventory of the Will Rogers Library. Among the missing volumes was a copy of Benjamin Franklin's *Poor Richard's Almanack and Other Papers*, which had been signed by someone named "Tate" and apparently sent to Will Rogers on March 31, 1925.
4. See Vernon Louis Parrington's insightful discussion of the significance of the Hartford Wits in his book, *Main Currents in American Thought.* Volume I, pages 364–374. Parrington is quite sympathetic with the plight of Trumbull, Dwight, Barlow and the other writers who were known as the Hartford Wits. He is also convinced that they worked diligently to save "the commonwealth of Connecticut from the pollutions of democracy." Still, Parrington, like almost every other cultural historian who has written about the Hartford Wits, concludes that their literary ambitions far exceeded their literary skills.
5. Joel Barlow, *The Columbiad.* Project Guttenberg, http://www.gutenberg.org.
6. One humorist who is extremely well represented in the Will Rogers Library is Frank McKinney (Kin) Hubbard, whose books such as *Abe Martin's Town Pump* (1929), *Abe Martin's Broadcast* (1930), and *Abe Martin Hoss Sense and Nonsense* (1926) utilize a voice that is similar to the voice of Will Rogers's Oklahoma cowboy persona. In addition to the folksy humor, the appeal in Martin's books is to "common sense" or "plain senses." There are close to ten volumes of Hubbard's writing in the Abe Martin persona in the Will Rogers Library. They have many marks and underlined portions that seem to indicate that Will Rogers may have either read them or at least used them as reference sources as he developed his own humorous monologues and newspaper articles.
7. The mere fact that Will Rogers attempted to acknowledge virtually every book he received in the mail from his many fans and admirers reflects the extent to which he

identified with common American men and women. Clearly, Will Rogers accepted this time-consuming task not only because he had great respect and compassion for average Americans, but he also wanted them to know he was not aloof and indifferent to their concerns. The many political books that were sent to Will Rogers during the Great Depression, for example, reflect the extent to which the American public identified Will Rogers with the plight of common Americans. Furthermore, his concern for these people was genuine—whether he identified them in his own voice, or in the voice of his Oklahoma cowboy persona.

8. At the risk of belaboring the point, the evidence in the Will Rogers Library—worn bindings, pencil marks in the margins, and underlining of passages—suggests that Rogers's satirical remarks on "book learning" were made more for the sake of "filling out" the character of the Oklahoma cowboy persona, than they were made out of any deep convictions on his part that book learning was always an inferior way of learning. Although Will Rogers may have read few books from cover to cover (with the exception of western novels, which he loved to read), he obviously used books to research many subjects that would become the foundations of his monologues and/or newspaper articles. The humorous books in his library are examples of this. Other examples involve the many travel books in the library, which also appear to have been well-used during his travels to foreign countries and, perhaps, even in his newspaper articles. During these travels, as in so many of his other activities, Will Rogers appears at times to conscientiously research and prepare his materials to achieve the natural, apparently effortless manner of writing and speaking that he favored in his Oklahoma cowboy persona.
9. There are at least four items in the Will Rogers Library that demonstrate Ben Franklin's pervasive influence over, and continued presence in American history and popular culture. The library contains Will Rogers's personal copy of the *Declaration of Independence*, which Ben Franklin helped to draft. The library has a set of *McGuffey's Readers*, which reflect many of Ben Franklin's ideas on education. The library has a copy of Emily Post's book on *Etiquette*, many of the ideas of which can be traced back to Franklin's similar writings on proper etiquette and decorum. And the library also has a 1926 edition of *The Encyclopedia Americana*, the format for which was inspired in part by Franklin's writings and publishing activities in a similar genre. Although the presence of these works in the library does not prove that Will Rogers read these twentieth-century recycled versions of the wit and wisdom of Ben Franklin, they do prove that virtually every American has consciously or subconsciously felt the influence of Franklin in their respective lives. And Will Rogers, who was more attuned than most of us to the forces that have shaped American culture, would inevitably have felt the pervasive presence of Ben Franklin in his life and surroundings.
10. F. Scott Fitzgerald, *The Great Gatsby.* (New York: Charles Scribner's Sons, 1925) 174–175.
11. There are an extremely large number of novels and other books about western history in the Will Rogers Library, and many of them were apparently acquired by Will Rogers himself. Even those friends and personal acquaintances who claim that Will Rogers was not much of a reader have to admit that western fiction and

nonfiction were of great interest to him. In western fiction, especially, he would inevitably have encountered Franklin's "noble rustic" in a cowboy outfit. And Will Rogers's early reading habits, together with the contents of his library, suggest that he was surrounded by such books.

12. The February 16, 1970, memorandum written by Edward A. Earl, area manager of the Will Rogers State Historic Park, indicated that Benjamin Franklin's *Poor Richard's Almanack* was one of fifty-nine (59) books that were missing when the California State Parks conducted an inventory of the library.
13. Carl Van Doren, *Benjamin Franklin.* (New York: the Viking Press, 1938) 570.
14. Although Will Rogers tried to use humor to defuse the rising tensions in Europe and America, he was not oblivious to the menacing presence of Hitler in Germany. In March of 1935, a few months before his death, he returned from a seven-week vacation to publicly discuss Hitler and the increasingly militant attitudes of Germany. His library also contains several books on Adolf Hitler and the Nazi movement. One book in particular, *The Voice of Destruction*, contains several pencil marks he had made next to passages concerning various threatening, militant statements Hitler had made in the early 1930s.
15. Ernest Hemingway, "All modern American literature comes from one book . . . ," *Goodreads*, http://www.goodreads.com>quotes>161912-all-mod.
16. Ben Franklin, "Silence Dogood No. 4." *Anthology of American Literature I. Colonial Through Romantic*, George McMichael General Editor. Macmillan Publishing Co., Inc., New York: 1974. 273–276.
17. Will Rogers, "Will Rogers Says," *San Francisco Chronicle*, Sunday, July 03, 1932, 30.
18. Further substantiating the careful work and effort Will Rogers put into the development of his stage act, Homer Croy points out that "His jokes were not such casual, offhand remarks as his audience may have like to believe" (107). Croy refers to two wrinkled pieces of paper on which Will Rogers had written down several "Gags for Missing the Horses Nose." Clearly, Will Rogers worked hard to achieve the seemingly effortless, spontaneous delivery of his Oklahoma cowboy persona. It also seems clear from the gags which have been carefully written down on the two pages of paper that this persona was the result of both inspiration and much careful preparation and methodical attention to detail.

# V.

# HISTORICAL AND MYTHICAL FRONTIERS

WITH THE Louisiana Purchase and the Lewis and Clark Expedition in 1803, the frontier phase of American history, which was eventually to have a profound influence on Will Rogers's humor and satire, began in earnest.[1] No other country had ever experienced anything quite like the American frontier, with the possible exception of Australia. However, Australia became drier and more uninhabitable as the early explorers moved further west; [2] whereas in America there was an immense area of open, fertile land in the West. It began to attract people from all walks of life and from every region of New England and many countries in Europe. In time, this frontier experience played a significant role in defining and shaping both American culture and American humor.

For over a century, historians have discussed and often disagreed over the true meaning of the American frontier experience and how it influenced the development of our nation's cultural values. The debate is evident in articles like David Lamb's "Wild West Life: Sweet It Wasn't." Lamb introduces his analysis of the frontier with the following statement:

> The settling of the West is our oldest and most enduring legend. It transformed cowboys from tradesmen to folk heroes, turned villains into national celebrities and so shaped our self-image that the frontier became the metaphor for American values.[3]

After discussing the "romanticized view of the Old West" that included "tall cowboys and knightly deeds," Lamb argues instead that the historical and anthropological evidence suggest that "frontier life was violent, grueling, impoverished and often pitiful" (A1).

Lamb is reexamining an argument that first appeared in the 1890s, when Frederick Jackson Turner argued that the frontier experience was the single most significant event in our nation's history. In July of 1893, at a meeting of the American Historical Association, Turner presented a paper titled "The Significance of the Frontier in American History," which became popularly known as "The Frontier Thesis." In this paper, Turner argued against the idea that European values and institutions were the major forces that shaped American institutions and cultural values. Turner argued instead that American values and institutions were unique because they had been shaped primarily by the westward movement, and by the unique experiences the American people encountered as they moved from one frontier to the next frontier until they had eventually journeyed across the entire continent.

Turner wrote, "American development has exhibited . . . a return to primitive conditions on a continually advancing frontier line . . . [and] this expansion westward with its new opportunities, its continuous touch with the simplicity of primitive society, furnish the forces dominating American character."[4] Turner also defined the frontier as a "gate of escape," which suggested that the immense area of land in the West had provided an escape valve for those Americans who wanted to flee from civilized constraints (38). Turner concluded that the frontier, except for certain areas in the Midwest, was, for all practical purposes, closed by the year 1893 (37–38). Although Turner argued that the American character was shaped by the frontier experience, he acknowledged that the American people eventually had to learn to live without the escape valve in the West that always held out the promise of a better life and a better future (37–38).

For a number of years after Turner presented his paper at the American Historical Association in Chicago, his ideas were widely accepted in scholarly communities. Almost every American historian tried to hook his or her own scholarly wagon to Turner's "Frontier Thesis." In time, however, the revisionist historians began to question Turner's thesis, and they challenged his assertions about the American frontier. They suggested Turner played much too loosely with the historical facts regarding life on the frontier. Some historians even accused Turner of writing fiction, when he should have been writing history.[5]

Other historians were more supportive, even though they too questioned many of Turner's assertions about the meanings of the American frontier. One of these historians, Henry Nash Smith, reevaluated Turner's Frontier Thesis in his classic study *Virgin Land, the American West as Symbol and Myth* (1950). Smith argued that the major problem with Turner's Frontier Thesis is that it failed to carefully distinguish between *myth* and *history* in his discussion of the American frontier. According to Smith, Turner thought he was writing about history, when he was actually writing about myth. Nonetheless, Smith concedes that the myths about the frontier experience are as important as the historical facts in explaining the development of American institutions and cultural values.

According to Smith, Turner's Frontier Thesis:

> Could hardly have attained such universal acceptance if it had not found an echo in ideas and attitudes already current. Since the enormous currency of the theory proves that it voices a massive and deeply-held conviction . . . [that] Americans of the present day cherish, an image that defines what Americans think of their past, and therefore what they propose to make of themselves in the future.[6]

Although Smith concludes that Turner was writing about a series of cultural myths regarding the westward movement, he nonetheless agrees that these myths, regardless of whether or not they are based on historical facts, are deserving of serious study because they reveal how Americans view themselves:

> Whatever the merits of the Turner thesis, the doctrine that the United States is a continental nation rather than a member with Europe of an Atlantic community has had a formative influence on the American mind and deserves historical treatment in its own right (4).

In the last chapter, Smith concluded that these myths about the frontier accompanied every stage of our nation's westward expansion and seemingly grew stronger and more compelling as the American population moved relentlessly across this continent. According to Smith, in the years following the closing of the frontier, a pervasive nationwide nostalgia set in, further perpetuating these myths and integrating them more fully into the historical realities. In time, the frontier myths and frontier history—especially the escape valve theory—became virtually inseparable. This was true even for Buffalo Bill Cody and other frontiersmen turned actors, who had first-hand experiences of what life had truly been like on the American frontier (291–305).

Although many of Frederick Jackson Turner's assertions in the Frontier Thesis were dismissed or modified by the twentieth-century revisionist historians, he nonetheless raised some fundamental questions. To what extent is American culture an extension of the European tradition? And to what extent is American culture a product of our nation's unique experiences on the western frontier? He may have erred on some specifics, but in retrospect there is considerable evidence to suggest that something unique was happening in this country from the years 1803–1890. Clearly, that something was westward expansion, and it was having a profound effect on the development of American cultural values and how we view ourselves as a nation.

No other country had ever moved across a continent as fast as America did in the nineteenth century. No other country had such an opportunity to abandon or greatly modify ancestral traditions. Even Frederick Jackson Turner's critics admitted that some uniquely American humorous and satirical traditions evolved out of the frontier experience. Perhaps it would be more accurate to say that American humor, once Ben Franklin reshaped it out of the remnants of a Puritan culture, assumed its uniquely "American" character during the nineteenth-century frontier experience.

As M. Thomas Inge points out in an "Introduction" to his book of essays, *The Frontier Humorists* (1975), this emerging native tradition of humor and satire did evolve out of the frontier experience, and it was significantly different than its European counterpart:

> It was the presence of the frontier that enabled the Americans to turn their eyes from Europe and see something uniquely their own.

> As the frontier advanced westward, as civilization came face to face with wilderness and savagery, the influence of Europe waned, and the American character took on new and independent outlines. Frederick Jackson Turner wrote in 1893 that "The frontier is the line of most rapid and effective Americanization." And although his sweeping generalization—that "to the frontier the American intellect owes its striking characteristic"—has been critically challenged, certainly much of what he says does seem to account to a large degree for the specific nature of Southwestern [frontier] humor.[7]

The fact that dramatic changes were sweeping across America during the years 1803–1890 is also apparent in the demographic evidence. The *Chronicle of America* (1990) reports that in the year 1800 there were 5.3 million Americans, with Virginia (807,557) being the most populous state, followed by Pennsylvania (602,365) and New York (589,051). The states of Ohio (45,365), Alabama (1250), and Mississippi (7,600) were located on the edge of the frontier when the census was taken in the year 1800 (224). By 1850, one year after gold was discovered in California, there were 23.2 million Americans in those areas. New York, Boston, Philadelphia, and Baltimore were still major population centers, but a radical shift was obviously underway as Americans moved "into virgin territory" in record numbers, thus establishing a greatly expanded frontier (339). By 1850, the American population was also becoming more decentralized, as evidenced by the following census statistics: California (92,957), Oregon (12,093), Texas (212,592), Utah (11,380), Mississippi (605,000), Missouri (682,000), and Wisconsin (305,391). By 1890, the nation's population had swelled to 63 million people. New York was still the most populous state, but all the "western states . . . [had] shown steady growth," with California's population topping "one million for the first time" (484).

The significance of this is that so long as America was a group of relatively self-contained colonies or states located on the eastern coast and in close proximity to the European trade routes, it was much easier for the European cultural traditions to assert themselves in the New World.[8] Once the decentralizing process began, and the American people in record numbers moved into the western territories, they were no longer in such close, daily contact with the European cultural traditions. Under these conditions, the European traditions no longer had such a stranglehold over the emerging native traditions, especially regarding humor. A truly American culture began to gain strength, one that had its roots in the values of the people who had first journeyed to America to establish Plymouth Plantation and Massachusetts Bay. But it was also an American culture that developed significantly different popular artistic and literary forms than anything ever experienced in Europe or the New England states, with the possible exceptions of what Ben Franklin had accomplished in his satirical and humorous writings.

Americans on the western frontier were obviously too far removed from theaters, art museums, libraries and other centers of high culture to make them the centers of their own lives. But they were not too far removed from the newly emerging frontier storytelling traditions. Nor did they need any special apparatus on the western frontier to participate in these forms of storytelling. The only requirement was that there had to be two people, and one had to have a story to tell. Nothing could be simpler.

By 1879, when Will Rogers was born in the Oklahoma territories, the storytelling tradition in America, and especially on the frontier, had been elevated to the status of a popular art form. It was our most unique popular art form, for it had been created primarily by common people who journeyed into the western territories. Although these people probably never completely severed ties with their European cultural traditions, they nonetheless developed a unique set of values and some unique forms of storytelling.

To place this in the context of Will Rogers's life and career, we should remember that although the American frontier experience is frequently described as a "gradual westward movement," it was in reality neither quite so "gradual," nor was it always a consistently "westward movement." It is true that after the Lewis and Clark Expedition (1803–1805) there were several decades of gradual westward expansion. However, after the discovery of gold in California in 1849, the frontier suddenly leaped over the middle of the continent and established itself farther west. Toward the latter part of the nineteenth century, as Turner suggests in the Frontier Thesis, the last frontier in the United States was located in the

Midwestern territories, which, of course, are precisely where Will Rogers spent his childhood and teenage years.[9]

Will Rogers (1879–1935) was born and raised in the Oklahoma territories, which did not even become a state until November 16, 1907. He experienced first-hand both the historical realities of frontier life and also the many myths that had accompanied our nation's westward expansion. In time, he learned to successfully integrate those historical facts and myths into his Oklahoma cowboy persona.

In her book, *Will Rogers, His Wife's Story* (1941), Betty Rogers describes her own initial reaction to the frontier community of Oologah, Oklahoma, where she was later to meet and marry Will Rogers: "the buildings were scattered along on each side of a single main street until it gave up being a street and dwindled out into a dim trail over the rolling prairies. There was not a tree in sight and the country seemed desolate and barren to a girl who had been raised in the ruggedness of northwestern Arkansas."[10] Spi M. Trent, writing in his book *My Cousin Will Rogers* (1938), responded to those people who wondered whether Will Rogers "was really raised on a ranch or was he just a drugstore cowboy . . . believe me he was a genuwine [*sic*] cowboy Roper and Rider from the time he was old enuff [*sic*] to straddle a horse."[11]

Others who did not know Will Rogers quite so intimately, but who were equally fascinated by both the man and his legend, are also convinced that the American frontier had an enormous influence on his life and values. Donald Day writes in the introduction to *The Autobiography of Will Rogers* (1949) that Will Rogers's sense of humor was inevitably molded by his early experiences in the frontier community of Oologah: "As the American frontier moved westward, the settlers listened more and more to horse-sense humorists . . . Will was born on the last frontier as it was passing out of existence. At his very doorsteps this unbelievable task of conquering a continent and building a great nation, in nothing flat as the lives of nations go, was being completed."[12] Richard M. Ketchum adds, in his book *Will Rogers, His Life and Times* (1973), that Will Rogers was "in the first place, a direct link to the original Americans—the Indians—and to the frontier that determined so much of the nation's history" (7). Similarly, in *Will Rogers: A Bio-Bibliography* (1984), Peter Rollins writes, "it was Rogers' self-appointed chore to test current fads, personalities, and events by frontier standards" (36). Rollins adds, "The symbolism of Rogers's death at the last point of land on the last American frontier was not missed by those who mourned [him]" (128).

Although the frontier may have closed by the last decade of the nineteenth century, the theme of the frontier as an escape valve—both as myth and historical fact—continued well into the twentieth century when Will Rogers was making his reputation as an entertainer. American literature, together with films and other forms of popular culture, made the escape-motif almost a national obsession. We became a nation of people whose values and perceptions of life had been molded by the myths and realities of the frontier experience. However, after the turn of the century, we no longer had a frontier into which we could escape. As a result, we created a group of restless, wandering literary protagonists, film characters, and mythologized historical figures who either remained constantly on the move, or in some very bizarre and occasionally self-destructive ways, tried to find a personal escape valve. If that escape was not to be found in the West, then it would have to be found somewhere else. The impulse to escape from the stifling constraints of civilized life and complexities was too strong to resist.

It was no accident that Will Rogers and other Americans in the nineteenth and early twentieth centuries were in the forefront of those people who sought to establish new frontiers in Alaska, Africa, the Arctic, and even the Antarctic. Nor was it an accident that Americans were the first to fly airplanes, cross the Atlantic Ocean in an airplane, or send a man to the moon.[13] The spirit of adventurism, together with the constant need to seek new frontiers, was by the twentieth century so ingrained in our character and sense of national purpose as to make us a nation of escape artists and risk takers. The American experience in the New World was one of constant movement, often pushing ahead into areas more sedentary nations, whose long histories were behind them, had lost the spirit to pursue.

American literature and popular culture also reflect this national yearning for a post-1890 escape valve. Sometimes it reflects negative, ritualistic, and even compulsive, destructive behavioral patterns in literary characters. Examples of the lingering national obsession with the frontier as an escape valve are everywhere in our literature and popular culture. Here are a few of many examples.

Scratchy Wilson, the last of a disappearing breed of cowboys in Stephen Crane's short story, "The Bride Comes to Yellow Sky" (1898), no longer has a frontier into which he can escape. Instead, he periodically engages in drunken, ritualistic reenactments of the original Wild West gunfights—even though he has no intention of harming anyone. When his old nemesis, Sheriff Jack Potter, who is newly married, refuses to take the bait and participate in yet another gunfight, Scratchy replies almost mournfully, "Well, I s'pose it's all off now." Scratchy's parting words not only refer to their ritualistic gunfights as he attempts to relive the "old days," they also refer to the closing of the frontier. Even his periodic drunken attempts to relive that past are now gone.[14]

Jay Gatsby, the surrogate son of Dan Cody (Wild Bill Cody!) in F. Scott Fitzgerald's *The Great Gatsby* (1925), tries to find an escape valve that will enable him to relive the past by establishing a relationship with the married Daisy Buchanan. He carries on with her as though nothing had changed since they parted several years earlier. Nick Carraway, the narrator, realizes at the end of the story that Gatsby's dream was connected to the original frontier experience. He concludes that Gatsby didn't know it "was already behind him, somewhere back in that vast obscurity beyond the city, where the dark fields of the republic rolled on under the night." Those "dark fields" are the prairie states where Will Rogers grew up (182).

R. P. McMurphy, in Ken Kesey's *One Flew Over the Cuckoo's Nest* (1962), is a man who remains constantly on the move to avoid the repressive forces of civilization. Later, he escapes into a mental institution, where he joins forces with Chief Bromden. Together, they become a modern version of the white man and his Indian companion we see so often in American literature and popular culture. Bromden has developed a schizophrenic escape valve into which he can flee whenever he is threatened by the forces of civilization, which he calls the "Combine." At the end of the story, when he makes his final escape from the mental institution, he tells the reader, "I might go to Canada eventually," which in his mind is the new frontier in the north.[15]

Similarly, Harry Angstrom, the "Rabbit" protagonist in John Updike's *Rabbit Run* (1960) and its sequels, hops about wildly and frantically from place to place as he tries desperately to escape from the tediousness of civilized life and his own responsibilities as a husband and father. The spirit of movement is alive inside of him, but there is no direction or purpose for his wanderings. So, he hops from place to place, and relationship to relationship, without purpose or meaning. The restless spirit of the original frontier is alive inside of him, but it is ultimately a self-destructive force that confines him to perpetual adolescence and an inability to accept adult responsibilities.[16]

It would be impossible to list all, or even a small percentage of films that have utilized the theme of a lost escape valve provided by the original frontier. Here are a few representative examples of films that reflect different takes on this theme. *Butch Cassidy and the Sundance Kid* (1969) follows the exploits of two frontier outlaws who must flee to Bolivia when lawmen finally catch up with them in the vanishing western American frontier. In Bolivia, however, their escape proves futile when police and soldiers trap them in a small courtyard and kill them. *Urban Cowboy* (1980) tells the story of an entire community of Texas oil workers and their wives and girlfriends who congregate at night in a Houston bar to compete for prizes by riding a mechanical bull. Although they compete in earnest, their efforts to ride the bull seem almost to be a parody of the horses earlier cowboys rode on the open range. *The Grey Fox* (1982) tells the story of a career criminal who can't give up his almost compulsive need to rob stagecoaches. After he is caught and spends twenty years in prison, he joins the modern world by robbing trains, not stagecoaches, until he is caught again. Finally, he makes another prison break and is rumored to have escaped to Europe, an ironic contrast to what was once considered the original escape valve in the American West. Another western, *Dances with Wolves* (1990), tells the story of a wounded Civil War veteran who flees to the western frontier where he hopes to heal both physically and emotionally. He eventually rejects the white man's world and joins a Native American tribe, thus severing all ties with the civilization that had mythologized the escape valve on the western frontier.

Will Rogers's perceptions of life were similarly molded by both the history and myths of the nineteenth-century frontier experience.

Beginning in his youth and continuing into his adult life, he was a man who tried to find some escape valve into which he could flee when he was overwhelmed by his own fame and the encroaching forces of civilization. Early in his life, he tried to escape through his constant travels throughout the world. Before he was thirty years old, he had already visited and performed in Argentina, South Africa, and many European countries.

Sedentary behavior was not compatible with his restless, wandering spirit. Like some early version of R. P. McMurphy in Kesey's novel, Will Rogers was an obsessive-compulsive traveler right up to the time of his death at the age of fifty-five, when his adventures with Wiley Post in Alaska also constituted a kind of escape into a last frontier. Although he was more stable and levelheaded than many of the other "compulsive travelers" in American history, literature, and film, he was seemingly every bit as obsessed with finding a personal escape valve to replace the one that had disappeared with the closing of the original western frontier on which he had been raised.

The Oklahoma cowboy persona provides another perspective on this same theme. This persona remains one of American culture's richest and most artistic interpretations of the escape-motif associated with the original frontier experience. Through the Oklahoma cowboy, Will Rogers implied many things about early twentieth-century American life. One of these insights involved his own growing awareness that, with the closing of the western frontier, real escape was no longer possible. The escape-motif could only be acted out ritualistically and symbolically on stage through rope tricks, or in films by riding off into the sunset. However, the Oklahoma cowboy and his rope tricks and stories were also symbols of hope for the many displaced country people in the audience. If it was possible for an Oklahoma cowboy to adjust to newly urbanized America without losing himself or his sense of humor in the process, then perhaps anyone could make such an adjustment. It just took a little time and a lot of ingenuity.

Will Rogers, growing up as he did on the Oklahoma frontier, would certainly have experienced the historical realities of what life had really been like in the West. His artistic sensitivities and intuitive responses to American cultural values would also have enabled him to understand the many myths associated with the frontier experience. Much of his success as a humorist and satirist was due to the fact that he so clearly and artistically integrated both myth and history into his Oklahoma cowboy persona until they became, like the myths and history of the original frontier itself, virtually inseparable.

Had his audiences sensed that they were merely watching an artificial symbol of the frontier myth, like some of the western heroes in Grade-B films, they might have dismissed the Oklahoma cowboy persona as a mindless fantasy suitable mostly for children. On the other hand, had they sensed that they were watching a historically realistic version of the Oklahoma cowboy in all of his tedious working-class authenticity, it is doubtful this character could have sustained sufficient audience appeal to have survived even the Ziegfeld Follies. Nor would he have appealed to the much larger national stage provided by the electronic media. It was Will Rogers's clever, seamless integration of both myth and historical reality into the Oklahoma cowboy persona that enabled him to unleash his audience's imaginations and allow their thoughts to drift back to an earlier time in American history. A time in their imaginations that was simpler and seemingly more hopeful.

In his book, *Virgin Land: The American West as Symbol and Myth* (1950), Henry Nash Smith points out that the myths regarding the American frontier were eventually commercialized and made available to an immense reading audience through the extremely successful popular cultural tradition of the western or dime novels. These novels, which were first published by Erastus Beadle in June of 1860, had been inspired by the noble, leather-clad frontiersman hero of James Fenimore Cooper's *The Leatherstocking Tales* (Smith, 99). In time, as competitors entered this lucrative commercial field, these novels incorporated "circus tricks of horsemanship, incredible feats of shooting, [and] more and more elaborate costumes" (101–102).

If we eliminate the "elaborate costumes" and substitute "roping" for "shooting," these literary devices are reminiscent of some of the elements Will Rogers later incorporated into his Ziegfeld Follies act. As Peter Rollins points out in his book *Will Rogers: A Bio-Bibliography* (1984), Rogers and his "cowboy friends were avid readers of pulp Westerns [like] Charles Siringo, *Fifteen Years on the Hurricane Deck of a Spanish Pony*" (126). Rollins concludes that "Such evidence seems to point to an intertwining of myth and reality even for cowboys 'round the campfire" (126).

Will Rogers undoubtedly modeled his Oklahoma cowboy persona in part on the heroes in these western or dime novels that preserved some of the hopes and fantasies of the original frontier.[17] This persona was not only one he was already comfortable with and had grown into because he had incorporated it into his own views of the West at a very young age. It was also a stage character he knew his audiences would recognize, since many of them had undoubtedly also read the dime or western novels. As Philip Durham and Everett L. Jones point out in an introduction to a collection of stories titled *The Western Story, Fact, Fiction, and Myth,* "The Western story is a special kind of popular literature that always commands a large audience."[18] Furthermore, Durham and Jones argue that this "seemingly endless outpouring of American Westerns" has had a pervasive influence on American culture and values:

> It is significant that no other part of our history becomes part of the play of children. Although simulated coonskin caps were once briefly sold to exploit the ephemeral popularity of a single Davy Crockett television series, they were quickly discarded. No child buys tricornered hats or Civil War costumes. Only pint-size Stetsons and toy six-shooters are perennial costuming staples in our toy shops (5).

When these children become adults, they still retain the subliminal memories they associate with the Western experience as it was popularized by the original dime novels, and later by the twentieth-century western films and comic books. These memories would include a variety of emotions: nostalgia for their own lost childhoods; freedom from adult responsibilities; and an unrequited longing and yearning for a simpler, more innocent world that had seemingly disappeared into the sunset along with the last covered wagon journeying into the West.

Will Rogers was not necessarily pandering to his audience's tastes in his stage act. His more historically realistic regalia was often a significant departure from the costumes worn by the cowboy heroes in the dime or western novels. He was nonetheless providing a stage image or symbol that would evoke various subliminal emotions in audiences that had inherited their views of the West from their childhood exposures to popular culture.

On stage, dressed in his battered hat, wrinkled shirt, bandanna, exposed shirt sleeves, leather chaps, and old boots, the Oklahoma cowboy twirled his rope majestically in undulating, rhythmic motions that elevated this working-class character to the status of myth, at the same time that his manner of dress kept him firmly grounded in historical reality. He became the symbol of the wistful illusions and grim realities of the last frontier: a bygone era that now existed only in the collective subconscious memories of the audiences that were mesmerized by the Oklahoma cowboy's rope tricks. The undulating rope, dancing a few feet above the stage, became a symbol of the freedoms that were once, but no longer, available to common people in the West. When the closed end of the loop settled over some stage prop or member of the audience, it reminded these city-dwelling, country people of the confinements, restraints, and limitations of newly urbanized America.

Twirling his rope like some stage hypnotist, the Oklahoma cowboy forced his audiences to search deeper and deeper inside of themselves for everything they associated with the western frontier: the dreams, the fears, the hopes, the nostalgia, the loneliness and despair, the sense of ever-longing for the unattainable. He brought back subliminal memories of everything the conduit of popular culture had taught them about our nation's frontier experience from the time they were very young. In the process, both the Oklahoma cowboy and his audiences were transported back in time to that faraway land out west, where the setting sun shines for those last fleeting seconds on the last American frontier.

After Will Rogers died, the images he had evoked about the West were so safely harbored in the hearts and minds of the American people, and so permanently enshrined in the sanctuaries of popular culture, that a grief-stricken public could scarcely find the strength or the words to say good-bye to their Oklahoma cowboy. As the hearse carrying Will Rogers's body moved slowly out of the Burbank, California, airport and slipped silently into the gathering twilight, a nation held its breath, unable to comprehend or accept the enormity of its loss. Will Rogers, in the guise of his Oklahoma cowboy, was not only their publicly anointed national humorist. He was also a living symbol of how life was, and how it might have been for all of the nation's common people on the last, now *lost* American frontier.

---

1. If there is a predominant theme running through the many volumes in the Will Rogers Library, it would have to be the "theme of the frontier." There are books with titles such as *Frontier Ballads, Frontier Fighter, New Frontiers, Oregon Trail Blazers, Life and Adventures of Buffalo Bill, Kit Carson Days,* and other volumes that directly or indirectly address the history and literature of the American frontier. Since most of these books were sent to Will Rogers by his many fans and admirers, it probably demonstrates how strongly the American people associated Will Rogers and his Oklahoma cowboy persona with the early years of the American frontier.
2. See the discussion of the Australian frontier in *The World Book Encyclopedia*, Vol. 1 (Chicago: Field Enterprises Educational Corporation, 1977) 895.
3. David Lamb, "Wild West Life: Sweet It Wasn't," the *Los Angeles Times* 27 April 1988: A1.
4. Frederick Jackson Turner, *The Frontier in American History* (New York: Henry Holt and company, 1921) 2–3.
5. See the collection of essays in John Francis McDermott's *The Frontier Re-examined* (Chicago: University of Illinois Press, 1967) and Michael P. Malone's *Historians and the American West* (Lincoln: University of Nebraska Press, 1983) for some responses to, and reevaluations of, Turner's Frontier Thesis.
6. Henry Nash Smith, *Virgin Land, the American West as Symbol and Myth* (New York: Vintage Books, 1950) 4.
7. M. Thomas Inge, "Introduction," *The Frontier Humorists* (Hamden, Connecticut: Archon Books, 1975) 1–2.
8. See the discussion of the development of early American colonial culture in Louis B. Wright's *The Cultural Life of the American Colonies, 1607–1763* (New York: Harper and Row, 1962).
9. See Frederick Jackson Turner's discussion of the last American frontier in the chapters titled "The Middle West" and "Middle Western Pioneer Democracy" from *The Frontier in American History* (New York: Henry Holt and Company, 1921).
10. Betty Rogers, *Will Rogers, His Wife's Story* (New York: The Bobbs-Merrill Company, 1941) 13.
11. Spi Trent, *My Cousin Will Rogers* (New York: G. P. Putnam Sons, 1938) 18.
12. Donald Day, "Letting Will Rogers Lasso Himself," *The Autobiography of Will Rogers*, by Will Rogers (Boston: Houghton Mifflin company, 1949) xiii-xiv.
13. The Will Rogers Library contains a number of books on the new Alaskan and other twentieth-century frontiers, with titles such as *Spell of the Yukon and Other Verses, Boating on the Yukon*, and *Outposts of Civilization*. There is an even larger collection of books on aviation, with titles such as *The Red Knight of Germany*, *Air*

*Travel, Around the World in 8 Days, This Aviation Business, World's Wings*, and other volumes. Since most of these books were sent to Will Rogers by either the authors or his fans, they demonstrate once again how closely the American people associated Will Rogers with both the old frontiers in the West and the new frontiers in Alaska and elsewhere. Clearly, for both Will Rogers and the American people, aviation opened up the new frontier in the sky in the same way that the Louisiana Purchase had opened up the old frontier in the West.

14. Stephen Crane, "The Bride Comes to Yellow Sky," *Great Short Works of Stephen Crane*, Harper and Row Publishers, New York (1965) 324.
15. Ken Kesey, *One Flew Over the Cuckoo's Nest*," Signet: The New American Library (1962) 272.
16. John Updike, *Rabbit Run*, Alfred A. Knopf (1962).
17. There is a large collection of western novels in the Will Rogers Library. These novels were written by authors who are the direct descendants of the writers of the dime or western novels of the type Will Rogers read when he was a young boy. These books include Zane Grey's *The Light of the Western Stars* and *Riders of the Purple Sage*, Harold Wright's *When a Man's a Man*, and many other western novels. There is an equally impressive collection of nonfiction books on the history of the American West. These books include works in the broad categories of western frontier history, California history, Oklahoma history, and Cherokee Indian history. Many of these books (both fiction and nonfiction) contain Will Rogers's personal signature and other marginal notes and evidence that indicate he probably acquired these books himself and used them in his stage and literary work. The intermingling of both myth and history in the library holdings also reflects a similar intermingling in the development of the Oklahoma cowboy persona. This is not to suggest that Will Rogers developed this stage and literary persona out of the materials available to him in his personal library. Rather, he clearly developed the Oklahoma cowboy persona out of his own personal experiences on the frontier, together with his intuitive reading of American culture. But his more deliberate readings, especially in the western or dime novel genres, undoubtedly added certain dimensions and refinements to this stage and literary persona as it developed over a period of time.
18. Philip Durham and Everett L. Jones, "Introduction," *The Western Story, Fact, Fiction, and Myth* (New York: Harcourt Brace Jovanovich, Inc., 1975) 1.

# VI.

# FRONTIER HUMOR

IN ADDITION to his rope tricks, the other thing Will Rogers learned on the Oklahoma frontier was the art of storytelling. Storytelling was as intrinsic an art form on the American frontier as ballet or theater or opera were in New York and European cities. The frontier storytelling tradition undoubtedly began with the first two or more explorers who journeyed into the areas newly acquired from France in the Louisiana Purchase. What else was there for these explorers to do for entertainment at night except swap stories around the campfire? The campfire became a primitive theatrical stage on which the early frontier storytellers could display their considerable oratorical skills. They often tried to outdo one another in storytelling competitions to determine who could tell the most outlandish tall tale.[1]

Even when the frontier outposts were gradually transformed into small towns and rural communities, storytelling remained a prized art form. This was especially true in the local taverns and saloons, where a predominantly masculine audience swapped yarns and exaggerated accounts of their personal experiences on the frontier (72–73). There was, after all, very little that these frontier communities could turn to for entertainment. They had no theaters, no ballet, no literary societies, no opera, no orchestras—nothing that would constitute real culture in the traditional sense of the term. They had only their storytellers. The stories they told, and the literary devices they used to tell them, were handed down from generation to generation with as much pride as one might pass on a cherished heirloom to a son or daughter. In a very short time, these individuals elevated storytelling on the frontier to the level of an American art form—perhaps the most authentic of all American art forms because it was created by common people, not a cultural elite.

The best of these stories were told by, or based on the experiences of, the many bizarre characters who chose to flee into the escape valve in the West. These writers almost all wrote under pseudonyms such as "Josh Billings," "Artemus Ward," "Bill Arp," and other such literary personae. However, long before these storytellers came on the scene, Ben Franklin had established the native tradition in American humor and satire—the tradition that flowed very naturally into frontier humor.

In *America's Humor*, Walter Blair and Hamlin Hill wrote:

> Franklin was an early discoverer of the most enduring American comic type—the homespun, unlettered, but shrewd man of common sense—and our longest-lasting joke about that type. He was also, in many ways that heretofore have not been recognized, a pioneer in developing a form of humor that worked particularly well here—the tall tale (54).

Other researchers and scholars, such as S. S. Cox in an early book on American humor titled *Why We Laugh* (1876), agreed. Although Cox is disappointed that Franklin "stifled his humor in the Addisonian style," he nonetheless credits the colonial satirist with establishing the foundations of frontier humor: "There is much of Franklin's shrewd, practical humor disguised under the mask of Josh Billings."[2]

What, then, is "frontier humor," and how is it reflected in Sam Clemens, who is Will Rogers's most immediate cultural predecessor, and later in Will Rogers himself? Undoubtedly, there are almost as many definitions of "frontier humor" as there are people who wrote it. In his book, *Mark Twain's America* (1932), Bernard DeVoto warned his fellow historians that "Frontier life across a nation and during three generations was extraordinarily complex. The humor of frontiersmen grew out of life at every level, so that an attempt to find unity in it would be folly."[3]

In spite of DeVoto's warnings, it is helpful to establish some general definitions of "frontier humor" as yardsticks that we can use to understand the humor, and especially the literary personae Sam Clemens and Will Rogers created in their respective literary works. This is not to suggest that once we have established these general characteristics, we can use them to stereotype each of the frontier humorists as though they all belonged in the same generic mold. Most of the frontier humorists had stylistic quirks and idiosyncrasies that differentiated them subtly, and sometimes not so subtly, from others of their kind. Still, there are general characteristics of frontier humor that help to illuminate the major trends in the development of American humor and, more specifically, to enable us to understand precisely where Will Rogers fits into that tradition. A virtual chorus of authors, researchers, and scholars—some of whose books were in the Will Rogers Library—have weighed in on the role of the frontier in creating American humor.

Bernard DeVoto, although he cautions his fellow historians and scholars to avoid sweeping generalizations about frontier humor since it involves such a diverse group of writers and storytellers, nonetheless provides a definition in his book, *Mark Twain's America* (1932). Although DeVoto's definition appears to be deliberately ambiguous, he nonetheless identifies realism of character portrayals, local color, and journalistic brevity as three of the essential elements in frontier humor: "It is a narrative of a length dictated by the necessities of newspaper publication, usually based on the life immediately at hand, and working through the realistic portrayal of characters toward the desired end, laughter" (243). M. Thomas Inge, in an introduction to a book of essays titled *The Frontier Humorists* (1975), stresses that frontier humor has four major characteristics: it is written for predominantly "masculine" audiences; it focuses on "lower-class white settlers"; it involves a "willing suspension of morality"; and it celebrates the virtues of "individualism" (5). Franklin J. Meine, in an essay titled "Tall Tales of the Southwest" (1930), organizes the subject matters of the frontier humorists into several broad categories: sketches of local customs; courtships and weddings; law circuits and political life; hunting stories; oddities in character; travel; frontier medical stories; gambling; varieties of religious experience; and fights.[4]

Other scholars and authors also attempted to define the uniqueness of American frontier humor. Pascal Covici Jr., in an essay titled "Mark Twain and the Old Southwest," from *Mark Twain's Humor: The Image of a World* (1962), argues that frontier humor was "largely organized around two impulses: a need to belittle and a desire to report."[5] Covici believes that much frontier humor involves "Brutality and coarseness . . . violence and exaggeration . . . [and an] impulse toward realism, toward a faithful presentation of the life of the region" (234). Andrew Lang, in "American Humor," from the book *Lost Leaders* (1889), argues that "Two remarkable features in American [frontier] humor . . . are its rusticity and its puritanism . . . The humorists are Puritans at bottom, as well as rustics . . . There is a kind of audacity in their use of the Scriptures, which reminds one of the freedom of mediaeval mystery-plays."[6]

In an essay titled "A Retrospect of American Humor" originally published in 1901, W. P. Trent, another researcher, writes of frontier humor:

> It is, on the whole, a broad humor that frequently does not disdain the aid of bad spelling and bad puns. It deals in incongruities of expression; it accentuates oddities; it sets the commonplace in ridiculous relief; it burlesques pretensions; it laughs at domestic, social, and political mishaps, when they are not too serious; it makes a game of foibles and minor vices; it delights to shock . . . but avoids all real grossness; it sometimes approximates sheer though innocuous mendacity.[7]

Joel Chandler Harris, in "Humor in America" (1909), argues that frontier humor is primarily an *oral*, not a *literary* tradition, and it was produced primarily by common people: "Much that is best and most characteristic about American humor has never had the advantage of type and binding. Much has been lost, but much has been preserved in the oral literature of the common people."[8] In *The World's Wit and Humor: American* (1906), Harris adds, "The fact remains that the vernacular, as distinct from literary form and finish, is the natural vehicle of the most persistent and most popular variety of American humor: hence the employment of what is frequently called dialect."[9]

In an essay titled "An American Comic Character" (1925), Jennette Tandy writes that frontier humor is normally told through the point of view of "a folk-hero, the homely American"; it focuses on "the provincial eccentricities of American life and the petty corruptions of American political intrigue"; and it utilizes "wise saws and rustic anecdotes and deliberately cruel innuendo."[10]

In "Our Native American Humor" (1936–1937), Sculley Bradley associates frontier humor with many of the simple virtues and strengths of character the original frontiersmen brought with them into the territories:

> Frontiersmen must live their lives with the mother of invention. They must be quick and cunning and strong. They must not be taken in by the appearance of things. They will come to value simple integrity of character and homely philosophy. As these attitudes grew in American thought they were reflected in American humor, and they still persist.[11]

Bradley adds, "Another element noted in our humor by the critical is its endless capacity for exaggeration" (66).

A somewhat different perspective is provided by Milton Rickels, who argues in "The Grotesque Body of Southwestern Humor" that one of the predominant characteristics of frontier humor is its obsession with physical deformities and crude references to various bodily functions: "The grotesque realism of Southwestern Humor includes, in addition to whole bodies, and the body undergoing accident, mutilation, and death, clusters of images around bodily processes: sexual activity; eating, drinking and digesting; and defecation."[12]

Still another perspective is offered by Leo Marx, in his book *The Machine in the Garden* (1967). Speaking specifically of Mark Twain's *Adventures of Huckleberry Finn* (1884) as a representative example of frontier literature, Marx suggests that this type of storytelling is frequently organized around the paradoxical themes of escape and entrapment. He argues that Huck, who is compelled "to forsake the benefits of civilization," flees first to Jackson Island, "another of those enchanting pastoral oasis so endlessly fascinating to the American imagination"; and later he flees down river with Jim, where the "idyll is not ended: the raft becomes a mobile extension of the island."[13] Huck and Jim are reenacting the same spirit that motivated the original explorers to seek freedom in the West. The irony is that, unbeknownst to them, they are escaping deeper into slave territory where there are even fewer freedoms, especially for men like Jim.

Commenting on the structure of many of the frontier tales, Walter Blair writes, in *Native American Humor* (1937), that one of the predominant characteristics of frontier humor is the tale, and the circumstances surrounding the telling of the tale are set up through a succession of first-person narrators who may, along with the reader, become the victims of the satire. This device, which is known as a "box-like structure" or "frame," does the necessary scene-setting until the teller of the tale is identified: "The story-teller would begin slowly, philosophizing, perhaps, as if he had no intention of telling a tale, but incidentally introducing his characters and meandering up to the beginning of the events he described" (91). The advantage of this structure, according to Blair, is that "it seemed artless . . . [and] gave an impression of naturalness" (92).

Another advantage to this strategy is the author disappears behind the narrator or narrators who establish the frame for the story. Perhaps, Blair suggests, nothing is quite so characteristic of the frontier humorists as their desire to conceal their true identities and intentions behind the literary personae they establish in their respective tales. Blair identifies over one hundred American humorists, including virtually all of the frontier humorists—storytellers such as Henry Wheeler Shaw (Josh Billings), Charles Farrar Browne (Artemus Ward), and Sam Clemens (Mark Twain)—who consistently used pseudonyms to establish literary personae that conceal their respective presences in their tales and stories (559–561).

Elsewhere, Blair identifies the following three forms of "Incongruity" that he believes are central to frontier humor:

- Incongruity between the grammatical, highly rhetorical language of the framework on the one hand and, on the other, the ungrammatical, racy dialect of the narrator.

- Incongruity between the situation at the time the yarn was told and the situation described in the yarn itself.

- Incongruity between realism—discoverable in the framework wherein the scene and the narrator are realistically portrayed—and fantasy, which enters into the enclosed narrative because the narrator selects details and uses figures of speech, epithets, and verbs which create grotesque images (92).

Constance Rourke, author of *American Humor: A Study of the National Character* (1931), provides yet another perspective on the frontier humorists. She argues that they were not so much focused on America's future, as one would expect in a nation caught up in the boisterous excitement and enthusiasm of Manifest Destiny, but rather on its past. According to Rourke, these writers made a "concerted effort to recover the past," the materials of which they would then turn into their tales and stories (181). In the process, these writers focused the nation's attentions not so much on *new frontiers*, but rather on the *last frontiers*, which probably accounts for the nostalgia and melancholy that one senses even in their most satirical and humorous writings (181–182). Rourke implies that this characteristic of frontier humor undoubtedly reflects the American tendency to consistently idealize the past—especially the frontier past, since each new frontier that was established as our nation surged across this continent unleashed great excitement. But it also unleashed a sense of nostalgia and lost expectations for the frontiers that had already been conquered.

If we organize these various observations regarding frontier humor into three categories—the speaker, victim, and story—we can make some broad generalizations about this popular American art form. Still, we should note again that there is considerable diversity in the ways the frontier humorists utilize these storytelling devices.

## GENERAL CHARACTERISTICS OF FRONTIER HUMOR

### *The Speaker:*

* is usually a literary persona and not the author
* insists the story is true, even if (especially if!) it couldn't possibly have happened
* must appear to be an "original"—someone who has no apparent cultural, historical, or ancestral antecedents
* appears to be simple, but is really a complex character who seldom reveals his true personality
* is an escape artist who is constantly fleeing from the forces of civilization
* is semiliterate or illiterate

* is seemingly unemotional
* comes from the lower classes
* is homely, physically unappealing, or somehow physically deformed
* is a country-bred character who appears to be ignorant, perhaps even a bumpkin or buffoon
* may, however, indirectly reveal much wisdom and common sense
* has little formal education
* is opposed to book learning and believes that experience is the only teacher—which is frequently the central theme of the tale
* is an obsessive and irrepressible practical joker
* may appear to be slightly deranged or mentally unstable
* is a deadpan satirist or poker-faced reporter who does not betray the fact that he knows he is telling a humorous story
* may be a harmless con-artist

*The Victim of the Satire:*

* is frequently set up by the speaker's "past victims" or other "locals" from the area
* is educated and literate
* is new in the area and uninitiated in the ways of frontier life
* uses Sandard English that is juxtaposed to the speaker's more vernacular speech patterns
* is knowledgeable in terms of book learning, but lacking in experience
* is eager to please
* lives in the city or in some other more civilized area
* is intelligent and sophisticated in civilized customs, but not country ways of doing things
* is naïve, gullible, and overly trusting
* belongs to a more respectable social class than the speaker
* can also be the reader if he or she accepts the speaker at face value
* is experiencing significant culture shock that will leave him confused, frustrated, and/or mystified by the strange, bizarre world he has entered

*The Story:*

* emphasizes the *manner* of telling the story rather than its *subject matter*
* is told with idiomatic expressions, rural dialects, and other forms of nonstandard English
* may have been told by the same speaker many times before, but must nonetheless appear to be spontaneous and extemporaneous
* must be told effortlessly and naturally, without apparent artistry or conscious craftsmanship
* must address an audience of average, common Americans
* must address a predominantly, if not exclusively, masculine audience
* frequently satirizes religious and/or biblical subjects
* must be kept reasonably short, as though it were written for a newspaper, although in some tall tales the speaker seems willing to ramble on forever
* may have been passed down through several speakers, each of whom added his own unique "style" to it
* frequently evokes in the audience a subliminal sense of nostalgia for "lost frontiers"
* has numerous diversions from the central storyline, many of which are more humorous than the story itself
* occasionally wanders around the outer peripheries of the central storyline without ever truly addressing the story
* must appear to be realistic and based on historical fact
* is a clear extension of the oral storytelling tradition in style and manner of presentation
* stretches the limits of traditional moral codes and acceptable manners of behavior
* builds from the plausible to any of several levels of absurdity, though the speaker never acknowledges the movement from the plausible and reasonable to the outrageous and absurd
* has not one, but many punch lines scattered throughout the story and especially in the diversions
* is frequently based on exaggeration in the tradition of the tall tale

* may involve seemingly deranged or physically deformed animals or human beings who nonetheless outwit their more intelligent adversaries

The earliest practitioners of frontier storytelling did not recognize its full potential. Nor should we have expected that they would. Nothing the human race has ever invented—radio, television, films, medical procedures, space travel, etc.—came into the minds of their earliest inventors fully developed. They had to be developed over time, usually by other inventive and talented people who built on those foundations and perfected them. Without the founders, however, there could be no such thing as art or science. It all had to start somewhere.

In the case of American storytelling, frontier humor came into existence spontaneously, created by average Americans who tried to find humor in the toils and struggles of everyday life. Often that humor helped them cope with the more burdensome responsibilities and disappointments of life on the frontier. It provided solace for the unexpected deaths and natural threats that challenged them daily. Once that foundation was in place, more talented writers could build on their storytelling skills—and they did.

In the writings of Will Rogers, we can see that he practices virtually all of these storytelling techniques, although he tends to avoid the crude and coarse implications of some of these strategies. His humor is usually witty, not cruel or belittling. However, he does use grammatically incorrect phrasing, inappropriate word choices, misspelled words, incorrect punctuation, illogical comparisons, and other strategies common among frontier storytellers.

The following brief comments Rogers made about horses demonstrate his method of gently chiding the victims of his satire, but usually without antagonizing or alienating them. Most of these comments, which are always kept short and written as though they come from an insightful but poorly educated speaker, address the virtues of horses over humans:[14]

## SUPERIORITY OF HORSES TO MODERN INVENTIONS

"There will never come a time when the old horse is not superior to any auto ever made."

"The country has gone sane and got back to horses."

"They used to take your horse and if they were caught they got hung for it. Now if they take your car and they are caught it's a miracle."

"Horses raise what the farmer eats and eats what the farmer raises . . . You can't plow in the ground and get gasoline."

## SUPERIORITY OF HORSES TO BIG BUSINESSES

"Legalize racing in every state. Sure people will bet, but they get to see the horses run and you certain can't see General Motors and General Electric and General Utility run when you bet on them."

## SUPERIORITY OF HORSES TO HUMANS

"Too bad, Australia . . . Phar Lap was just a horse but he brought you honor and represented you nobly."

## HORSES AS THE GREAT EQUALIZERS

"After seeing kids play polo against big guys, it only shows that horses are the greatest equalizer in the world. No matter what you weigh, the little fellow is your equal on a horse."

## HISTORY OF HORSEMANSHIP

"Horsemanship through the history of all nations has been considered one of the highest accomplishments . . . You can't pass a park without seeing a statue of some old

> codger on a horse. It must be to his bravery, you can tell it's not to his horsemanship."

## HORSES AND THE GREAT DEPRESSION

> "I love horses and I only ask—don't let me know which one we are eating today."

Will Rogers used the same short, colloquial, folksy style to comment on many other subjects. He demonstrated that he was a keen observer of human behavior and the many idiosyncrasies and imperfections that have plagued humanity throughout history. Here are some of his aphorisms and short, pithy statements that express these insights in the same style, point of view, and underlying common sense earlier frontier humorists used in their storytelling:

## POLITICS AND ELECTIONS

> "Elections are a good deal like marriages; there is no accounting for one's taste. Every time we see a bridegroom, we wonder why she ever picked him, and it's the same with public officials."

> "They talk about what a great thing the radio has been for politicians and candidates. Why, there has been more people got wise to over the radio than Senate investigations have exposed. Nothing in the world exposes how little you have to say as radio."

> "I've been trying my best to help Mr. Hoover and Wall Street 'Restore Confidence.' You take confidence, it's one of the hardest things in the world to get restored once it gets out of bounds."

> "Both sides just spent the whole summer hunting up things to cuss the other side on. That the other side might be right in a lot of things never entered their

head. In fact, they wouldn't let it enter it. A politician is now as narrow-minded as he forces himself to be."

## WARS

"I looked for combinations that were friendly toward each other and have yet to find one—unless it was Latvia up toward the Arctic Ocean and Madagascar down on the Indian Ocean. They have no particular grievance against each other but they will have as soon as they find where each other are."

## CRIME AND PUNISHMENT

"Crime today, say robbery, or some minor event, we fine them; and if it's confessed murder, why, they plead insanity. We go on the theory that if you confess you must be insane."

"Authorities having trouble rounding up twelve escaped lunatics. The main trouble is recognizing 'em. I bet they get a different twelve back in."

"Nowadays it's about as big a crime to be dumb, as it is to be dishonest."

## WOMEN AND MEN

"What's this generation coming to? I bet you the time ain't far off when a woman won't know any more than a man."

"Funny thing about the White House: It wears down the most hardy of our men folks, but women seem to thrive on it."

"Another American woman just now swam in from France. Her husband was carried from the boat suffering from cold and exposure. She has two children; the smallest a girl is swimming over tomorrow. Yours for a revised edition of the Democracy explaining which is the weaker sex."

EDUCATION

"America is becoming so educated that ignorance will be a novelty. I will belong to a select few."

"Does college pay? It does if you are a good open field runner!"

"Why don't they pass a Constitutional Amendment prohibiting anybody learning anything? And if it works as good as the Prohibition one did, in five years we would have the smartest race of people on Earth."[15]

Humor can be many things, and Will Rogers understood them as well as anyone who ever lived. Most of his humor is gentle. It pokes fun at the foibles of human nature that never change. Some of it is more serious. It addresses the dictators, tyrants, kings, and politicians that have plagued the human race since we first set foot on this small planet. Whatever the subject, Rogers encourages us to be better than we are by examining our limitations through laughter.

He never saw the horrors of World War II. Nor did he see the mushroom clouds over Hiroshima and Nagasaki that ushered in a new era when life on this planet could be extinguished in a few short hours. But he did not live in a world without human tragedies and natural disasters.

What he taught us was how to live with the frailties of human life and turn them to laughter. He understood, more than most people, that we need to learn to live together, and maintaining a sense of humor is the balm that often makes this possible.

---

1. Walter Blair, *Native American Humor* (San Francisco: Chandler Publishing Company, Inc., 1960) 72.

2. S. S. Cox, "*From Why We Laugh* (1875–1976), "*Critical Essays on American Humor*, ed. William Bedford Clark and W. Craig Turner (Boston: G. K. Hall & Co., 1984) 25–26.
3. Bernard DeVoto, *Mark Twain's America* (New York, 1932) 241.
4. Franklin J. Meine, "Tall Tales of the Southwest," *Critical Essays on American Humor,* ed. William Bedford Clark and W. Craig Turner (Boston: G. K. Hall & Co., 1984) 24–25.
5. Pascal Covici Jr., "Mark Twain and the Old Southwest," *Critical Essays on American Humor,* ed. William Bedford Clark and W. Craig Turner (Boston: G. K. Hall & Co., 1984) 234.
6. Andrew Lang, "From 'American Humor' (1889)," *Critical Essays on American Humor*, ed. William Bedford Clark and W. Craig Turner (Boston: G. K. Hall & Co.,1984) 31.
7. W. P. Trent, "A Retrospect of American Humor [1901]," *Critical Essays on American Humor*, ed. William Bedford Clark and W. Craig Turner (Boston: G. K. Hall & Co., 1984) 38–39.
8. Joel Chandler Harris, "[From 'Humor in America' (1909)]," *Critical Essays on American Humor*, ed. William Bedford Clark and W. Craig Turner (Boston: G. K. Hall & Co., 1984) 46.
9. Joel Chandler Harris, *The World's Wit and Humor*: American (New York, 1906), I, xxii.
10. Jennette Tandy, "An American Comic Character [From *Crackerbox Philosophers (1925)],*" *Critical Essays on American Humor*, ed. William Bedford Clark and W. Craig Turner (Boston: G. K. Hall & Co., 1984) 50.
11. Sculley Bradley, "Our Native Humor [1936–1937]," *Critical Essays on American Humor*, ed. William Bedford Clark and W. Craig Turner (Boston: G. K. Hall & Co., 1984) 64.
12. Milton Rickels, "The Grotesque Body of Southwestern Humor," *Critical Essays on American Humor*, ed. William Bedford Clark and W. Craig Turner (Boston: G. K. Hall & Co., 1984) 160.
13. Leo Marx, *The Machine in the Garden* (New York: Oxford University Press, 1967) 326–327.
14. Will Rogers Memorial Museum Archives, Claremore, Oklahoma.
15. The Will Rogers aphorisms have been selected from large collections available through the public domain.

# VII.

# WILL ROGERS AND MARK TWAIN

FROM THE time Will Rogers became famous, he inspired comparisons with Mark Twain. Those comparisons were perhaps inevitable, given the fame both men achieved in their own lifetimes. The ways these two humorists spoke to the nation were similar in some respects, and yet often very different. Perhaps the most important connection the two humorists had in common was that both had their roots embedded deeply in the American frontier history and storytellers that preceded them.

When we address the life and writings of Sam Clements (1835–1910), alias Mark Twain, we are over two centuries removed from the original Puritan ventures in the New World. However, Twain had direct personal connections to the theological extremes of the early Puritans through his mother, Jane Clements. Albert Bigelow Paine describes her as a "charitable, sympathetic woman . . . [but] her religion was of that clean-cut strenuous kind which regards as necessary institutions hell and Satan."[1]

Twain's mother clung to these beliefs, while paradoxically sharing with her son a deep love for storytelling and joke-telling. She was living proof that a humorist could evolve out of a Puritan culture and a home that was still deeply entrenched in the biblical Old Testament accounts of Satan's intrusions into human affairs, the damned burning throughout eternity, and other such verbal descriptions of what awaited sinners in the afterlife. Twain eventually turned many of these rigidly doctrinal ideas into jokes in his writings and stage presentations.

The one area where Twain seemed to be in agreement with the original Puritans was their conviction that humans have a greater propensity for evil than good. During his long life, readers can sense in his writings a gradual drift toward a cynical condemnation of the human race. He still believed that there were good, kind souls like Huck and the slave Jim, but he became more convinced that they were becoming rarer.

Will Rogers, who came on the scene in 1879 and outlived Twain by twenty-five years, had no such direct Puritan theocratic presence in his life. The biblical threats of hell and eternal damnation were foreign to him. His view of human nature was much more forgiving and charitable. His reported claim, "I never met a man I didn't like," is probably overstated and taken out of context. However, he did not become the misanthrope Twain became in his later years. Rogers's connections to the early Puritan culture were more in their preference for the plain style, work ethic, and other simpler and less intrusive ideas.

What Twain and Rogers definitely shared is the influence of the history and myths of the American frontier experience. They were both deeply aware of their indebtedness to the early humorists who evolved out of the frontier storytelling traditions.

Most scholars tend to agree that Mark Twain, more than any other American writer or storyteller, elevated the elements of frontier humor to the level of an art form. M. Thomas Inge writes, "Of special significance to American literature . . . is the fact that in the early writings of Mark Twain, Southwestern [frontier] humor reached its climax and provided him with basic themes and techniques that he would masterfully use in his own works with a skill and brilliance undreamed of by the frontier humorist[s]" (8). Pascal Covici writes, "to understand Mark Twain's use of humor, is, at least partly, to put oneself in tune with the early frontier and western humor of America" (233). According to Covici, Mark Twain's genius is that he "Americanizes American humor," especially in his classic novel, *Adventures of Huckleberry Finn* (240).

Mark Twain is the most important bridge between the original American Puritans in the seventeenth century, Ben Franklin in the eighteenth century, and Will Rogers in the early part of the twentieth century.[2] As we search for the ultimate source of American humor, we find the native tradition in American humor, as opposed to the inherited European tradition, developing along the following lines:

| American Puritans (17th Century) | → | Ben Franklin (18th Century) | → | Mark Twain (19th Century) | → | Will Rogers (20th Century) |
|---|---|---|---|---|---|---|

The Puritans did not reveal a sense of humor, and they often saw laughter as evidence of a weakened moral sense. However, in subtle ways their grim-faced, unemotional countenances and manner of conducting their lives probably inadvertently contributed to the later storytellers who refused to acknowledge that anything they said was funny.

Ben Franklin established a new foundation for American humorous storytelling. He did not make a complete break with the traditions of British satire, nor should we expect that he would. However, through characters like Silence Dogood, he established a new direction for American humorists to follow. In the process, he had a major influence on the development of the native traditions in American humor.

Mark Twain also had such a profound influence on nineteenth- and twentieth-century American humor and culture that it would have been impossible for Will Rogers to avoid Twain's influence. Like Ben Franklin, who had taken certain basic ideas out of America's Puritan past and reshaped them to establish the foundations for the native tradition in American humor, Twain reshaped the frontier storytelling tradition into an art form. He had such a profound influence on American thought and values that his ideas were assimilated and passed from generation to generation through the conduit of popular culture.

Will Rogers was also closely acquainted with the frontier tradition in American humor, not only through his personal experiences while growing up in the Oklahoma territories, but also through direct experiences with Twain's written works. Peter C. Rollins reported that George Horace Lorimer, editor of the *Saturday Evening Post* and the man who suggested to Will Rogers on April 15, 1926, that he write a newspaper column, made direct reference to Mark Twain when he approached Rogers with a proposal. According to Rollins, "Lorimer wondered if Rogers could write a special feature series of weekly articles which would take a similar approach to the pressing foreign policy issues confronting the nation, something along the lines of Mark Twain's famous travelogue, *Innocents Abroad*" (44). Shortly thereafter, as Will Rogers began to write his newspaper column, he "put himself in the role of innocent abroad for both comic and serious purposes . . . Following Twain's example in *Innocents Abroad (1879)*, Rogers played upon the theme of the superiority of the American landscape" (44–47).

In *The Autobiography of Will Rogers*, Rogers reveals that he had more than just a passing acquaintance with both the life and literary career of Mark Twain. While describing a steer his father lost while transporting cattle across the Mississippi River, Rogers wrote: "He went on down the river and I don't know at that if he ever drowned. Mark Twain just liable to pick him up with one of those Mississippi steam shovels of his, on down the river someplace."[2] In the essay, "How to Be Funny," Rogers also describes a would-be humorist from Lincoln, Nebraska, who asked him, "In training [to be a humorist] what should one aim for?" Rogers replied, "Aim for Mark Twain, even if you land with Mutt and Jeff."[3]

Rogers probably meant for his response to be somewhat flippant. However, it reveals his awareness that Mark Twain's literary works are the epitome of American humor. Twain had such an influence on our native traditions that his humor was virtually identifiable with American humor. The remark also implies that Will Rogers believed every American humorist could learn from Mark Twain, and even if they fell short, they would inevitably write or say some things that are funny.

Will Rogers reveals a somewhat more complex attitude toward Mark Twain in a telegram he wrote to *The Hannibal Courier* on February 27, 1935. In his typically self-effacing style, Rogers declined the offer to be included in a planned edition of Mark Twain's writings because he did not consider himself to be in the same league with the great author and humorist. Although Will Rogers dismisses the idea that he is "the modern Mark Twain," the letter, with misspelled and probably deliberately incorrect word choices, again reveals that he has an intimate sense of, and appreciation for, Twain's contributions to American humor:

February 27 [telegram]:
*The Hannibal Courier*, Hannibal, Mo.

> I never did write you before because it seemed as redicilous [*sic*] for me to even get my name mixed in with a Mark Twain affair as for all the Kentucky Colonels to be asked to contribute to a war record memorial to Napoleon. Me in your Mark Twain edition would be like Sister Aimee being asked to the Lords Supper. Why I would be Huey Long in a Supreme Court robe. There is one thing that ought to be eliminated in this country and that is every time somebody gets a laugh of some small dimensions, why he is called the modern Mark Twain. Well you know when the Twain successor will appear in our country, there will be two of em, and they will arrive together, one will be to replace Abraham Lincoln, and the other to replace Mark Twain (*Autobiography, 370–71*).

This letter, especially the sentence that implies Mark Twain was the yardstick used in America to measure anyone who "gets a laugh of some small dimensions," reveals that Will Rogers may have had a somewhat ambivalent attitude toward the comparison with Twain. He probably sincerely believed that he was not worthy of those comparisons to the author who would be described as "the Lincoln of our literature."

There are, nonetheless, some areas in which the two humorists share personal histories. Mark Twain's death in 1910 unleashed an enormous amount of public grief and nostalgia for this cultural icon.[4] Ironically, this outpouring of grief and nostalgia was equaled, and perhaps even surpassed, twenty-five years later when Will Rogers died, an event that also devastated people all across America and the rest of the world.[5] Twain died on April 21, 1910, when Will Rogers was thirty years old. So there was considerable overlap between their two careers—even though Will Rogers was not yet a household name in 1910, whereas the name "Mark Twain" was known worldwide.

Will Rogers was genuinely willing to accept a small humorous niche for himself in the shadow of this literary giant. What he rejected was the idea that he should be cast in the role of the "modern Mark Twain," because he realized in some ways they were very different humorists. Although they both evolved out of the traditions established by the frontier humorists, they developed different styles and satirical strategies—as one would expect from two gifted humorists.

It is also important to note that Will Rogers played the lead role of "Hank Morgan" in the film version of Twain's *A Connecticut Yankee in King Arthur's Court* (1889), which was produced and copyrighted on February 25, 1931 (Sterling's *Hollywood*, 111). The early reviews of the film suggested that Rogers clearly understood the spirit of Twain's novel. *The New York Times*' review on April 19, 1931, stated, "Will Rogers suits the title role of the film of Mark Twain's *A Connecticut Yankee in King Arthur's Court* [*sic*] so well that when one picks up the book one instantly visualizes this recruit from the saddle and the plains" (112). Another review in *The New York Times*, dated March 2, 1934, stated, "As the Connecticut Yankee, he looked as though he had stepped out of Mark Twain's book. . . ." (137).

In spite of Will Rogers's self-effacing protestations, there is considerable evidence to suggest that he was greatly influenced by Mark Twain's life and career, as were all American humorists.[6] There is equally compelling evidence that Will Rogers is an extension of the frontier tradition in American humor that Twain refined and elevated to the level of an art form.

What precisely, then, is the relationship of Mark Twain's humor to Will Rogers's humor? How does their humor fit into the traditions established by the frontier humorists? And how does Mark Twain's humor enable us to better understand the development of Will Rogers's Oklahoma cowboy persona?

Comparisons of the satirical and humorous styles of Will Rogers and Mark Twain on similar subjects are revealing. Twain utilizes a tightly controlled style that does not add a single word or syllable more than is necessary to make his point. Will Rogers creates a looser, more relaxed style with many filler words and idiomatic expressions to create a gentler, folksier style. We should also note that Twain is deliberately writing aphorisms, whereas Rogers is writing his short newspaper columns in a series of sentences that often sound like aphorisms. Twain's satire is also more caustic, whereas Rogers is usually careful not to antagonize or alienate the target of the joke:[7]

## BOOK READING

"Books twice as good if they was half as big. Books twice as good if they was fifty percent less, and the ones left half as thick."—Will Rogers

"Classic. A book which people praise and don't read."—Mark Twain

"My books are like water; those of the great geniuses are wine. Fortunately everybody drinks water."—Mark Twain

## POLITICS

"I told you not to be too optimistic about the Senate resigning. They filibustered all last night. We pay for wisdom and we get wind."—Will Rogers

"Suppose you were an idiot, and suppose you were a member of Congress; but I repeat myself."—Mark Twain

## SELF-EFFACING HUMOR

"I am an awful windy old talker and my wife says I bore more people than I entertain. She says I can do more talking away from home and less at home than anybody, for then I bog down and get my nose in a paper."—Will Rogers

"I don't like to commit myself about heaven and hell—you see, I have friends in both places."—Mark Twain

## SATIRIZING CELEBRITIES

"It's as I have often said. You can always joke good naturedly a big man, but be sure he is a big man before you joke about him."—Will Rogers

"There is no distinctly American criminal class—except Congress."—Mark Twain

Some longer passages from the writings of Will Rogers and Mark Twain are equally revealing.

## "WILL ROGERS SAYS TODAY" COLUMN FROM JANUARY 14, 1928:

> "I found on my arrival in Washington that some people had censured me severely for leaving the impression that Mr. Coolidge was on the radio. Well, the idea that anyone could imagine it was him uttering the nonsense that I was uttering! Well, it struck me an insult to anyone's sense of humor to announce that it was not him. So I wrote Mr. Coolidge a note explaining, and, received a two-page letter within 30 minutes from him written all in his own longhand, saying 'that he had been told of it, but knew that anything that I did was done in good natured amusement, and to not give it, a moment's worry,' and also thanked me for my kind references to him on various occasions of which he had heard."[8]

Will Rogers's prose style has some minor verbal quirks, but it is still well within the rules of Standard English. The most obvious grammatical issue is the long run-on sentence that is spread over several lines of the text. In comparison, the opening paragraph of Mark Twain's *Adventures of Huckleberry Finn,* in which Huck introduces himself to the reader, virtually destroys Standard English.

## HUCK INTRODUCING HIMSELF TO THE READER IN *ADVENTURES OF HUCKLEBERRY FINN*:

> "You don't know about me without you have read a book by the name of *The Adventures of Tom Sawyer*, but that ain't no matter. That book was made by Mr. Mark Twain, and he told the truth, mainly. There were things which he stretched, but mainly he told the truth. That is nothing. I never seen anybody but lied one time or another, without it was Aunt Polly, or the widow, or maybe Mary. Aunt Polly—Tom's Aunt Polly, she is—and Mary, and the Widow Douglas is all told about in that book, which is mostly a true book, with some stretchers, as I said before."[9]

Huck is speaking in the only lower-class, semiliterate language he knows, and a good part of the humor in the story comes from the disparity between *what* he describes and *how* he describes it. We could point out the grammatical lapses—misspelled words, slang, coinages, awkward phasing, passive voice constructions, etc.—and the passage would probably have received a grade of F in the schools Ben Franklin attended. But that's the beauty of what Twain wrote. We revel in the joy of Huck's shattering of the rules of English grammar. It's what makes Huckleberry Finn so enjoyable to read.

Although the Hartford Wits attempted in the eighteenth century to write an American epic in the style of British epics and failed, a case could be made that Sam Clemens, through the persona of Mark Twain, is America's epic writer. An equally strong case could be made that *Adventures of Huckleberry Finn* (1884) is America's literary epic, much as the *Aeneid* was Rome's epic, and the *Iliad* and *Odyssey* were Greece's epics. Mark Twain, in *Huckleberry Finn,* unites virtually all of the general characteristics of frontier humor together with his own unique vision of America's values and culture. In the process he created a democratic epic with an authentic literary epic hero from the lower classes—Huck Finn himself. Twain deliberately chose Huck because he was uneducated and spoke in a dialect that separated American English once and for all from the English language we had inherited from Great Britain.

Although Will Rogers never wrote an extended work of literature, a strong case could be made that his Oklahoma cowboy, who is in some respects a twentieth-century, somewhat better educated, adult version of Huck Finn, was the closest thing to an epic folk hero this nation has ever produced. Although literary purists could counter that a character must appear in at least one major work of literature to qualify as an "epic hero," perhaps a democratic society has the right to broaden this definition. Furthermore, with the exception of Mark Twain, the frontier storytelling tradition did not, as a rule, create extended works of literature. Nor were the best of these stories necessarily typed and printed in literary form. The frontier humorists did, however, elevate the simple oral tradition of storytelling to the level of a popular art form.[10]

Will Rogers is an extension of that oral storytelling tradition. Through the Oklahoma cowboy persona, he gave that tradition historical and mythical dimensions that are almost epic in scope. Since Will Rogers accomplished this in the most representatively "American" of all art forms, the simple storytelling traditions of common and lower-class people, perhaps one could argue that his Oklahoma cowboy can also claim to be an American epic folk hero.

The literary personae Sam Clemens and Will Rogers created also had their differences, as one might expect from two storytellers with more than their share of quirks and idiosyncrasies. Perhaps the most obvious similarity is that, in the eyes of the American people, Sam Clemens and Will Rogers become indistinguishable from their public personae of "Mark Twain" and the "Oklahoma cowboy," respectively. However, even here there is a significant difference because most people would eventually have to concede that Sam Clemens and Mark Twain are ultimately two different people, if for no other reason than the mere fact that they have different names. Will Rogers never adopted a permanent pseudonym for his Oklahoma cowboy. The "Cherokee Kid" is probably the closest he ever came to such a pseudonym. Still, many people believe Will Rogers and the Oklahoma cowboy are the same person. The more one studies Sam Clemens and Will Rogers, however, the more one senses that they were both master actors in the best sense of the term. In the guise of their respective personae, they were on stage virtually all the time.

Photographs taken of the two authors during various stages in their lives and professional careers are revealing. Mark Twain, who was one of the most photographed men of his time, is remarkably consistent in terms of his facial expressions and demeanor. This is partly due to the posing techniques of the time, but there is nonetheless a consistent pattern with only a few exceptions. Sam Clemens—both before, during, and after he assumed the pen name of "Mark Twain"—almost never looks directly into the camera. He never smiles, and he almost never reveals his innermost emotions to the camera. In a series of photographs that are reproduced in *Cobblestone* (May, 1984), we can see a young Sam Clemens posing as an apprentice printer (9); as a young man who has just received his riverboat pilot's license (14); as a reporter on the *Territorial Enterprise* in Nevada (15); as a world traveler posing with his family on board a ship (28–29); and as an older man staring out the window on the front cover of the magazine. In none of these photographs does Twain smile or reveal any emotional responses to the events that are taking place around him.[11]

Similar patterns are obvious in photographs that are reproduced in Gladys Carmen Bellamy's book *Mark Twain as a Literary Artist* (1950).[12] In these photographs, we see Mark Twain posing again as a young man (18); as an amateur actor on stage (50); with George Alfred Townsend and David Gray (146); with a former slave (242); as a "saddened humorist" after the death of his wife and two of his daughters (274); on board ship with a young friend (306); in bed (338); and with his daughter Clara, the last surviving member of his family (370). Only in the photograph of Mark Twain on stage do we sense even the slightest glimmer of mirth, humor, or any other kind of emotion in his demeanor. Even the photograph of the "saddened humorist," who has just lost virtually his entire family, does not reveal much of the obvious grief, anguish, and torment that we know from his writings he must be feeling.

Sam Clemens, both in his youth and later when he assumed the persona of Mark Twain, is the epitome of the poker-faced reporter or storyteller who evolved first out of a Puritan culture, and later out of the traditions established by the frontier humorists. We know that Twain was a man who had deep emotions, a fact that is painfully obvious to anyone who has read the last chapter of his autobiography. In this often painful recollection of his life story, Twain reveals the overwhelming grief and anguish he experienced when his daughter Jean died tragically and unexpectedly, leaving him virtually alone in the world except for his last surviving daughter Clara who was in Europe.[13] Nothing in the private or public revelations of our nation's writers is quite as poignant, heart-wrenching, and emotionally exhausting as Twain's account of his attempts to carry on while his daughter's body lay in an adjacent bedroom during the Christmas season. Mark Twain was clearly a man who had deep emotions. But like his Puritan ancestors, and later the frontier humorists, he suppressed those emotions behind a literary persona that revealed little mirth or levity. Even in the photographs, he usually avoided any eye contact that might inadvertently reveal the person behind the persona.

Unlike Mark Twain and the other frontier humorists, Will Rogers is normally not a poker-faced reporter or storyteller, although he will use such strategies when they suit his satirical purposes. Through his

Oklahoma cowboy persona, he usually establishes a much warmer, more personal relationship with his stage, film, radio and/or newspaper-reading audiences. Photographs of Will Rogers must be taken in the context of contemporary posing techniques and the time, place, and circumstances in which he is being photographed. Nonetheless, they often reveal him or the Oklahoma cowboy as warmer and more caring, albeit also slightly whimsical.

In her book, *Will Rogers, His Wife's Story* (1941), Betty Rogers includes some early photographs of her husband, one titled "Will at twelve years" and the other "High Life at Kemper Military Academy" (39). In both photographs, Will poses much the same way Sam Clemens did in his early photographs. He neither makes eye contact with the camera, nor does he smile or reveal any emotions. He appears, instead, to be a well-mannered, albeit somewhat bored, young gentleman. In another photograph from Betty Rogers's book, this one an 1897 group photograph of the Kemper football team, a handsome young Will Rogers makes eye contact with the camera. However, he, along with the other players, neither smiles nor reveals any emotions (53). In a photograph taken in 1903, Will Rogers, who is billed as "the Mexican Rope Artist" and who is dressed somewhat like a bullfighter (perhaps another early experiment with an emerging persona) looks into the camera, but he still does not smile or reveal any emotions (102). In sum, these early photographs reveal Will Rogers to be a young man who might naturally have grown into the role of poker-faced reporter or storyteller, but we see little evidence to suggest that he carries inside of himself the ability to become the warm, engaging, whimsical Oklahoma cowboy of later years.[14]

Other early photographs in Betty Rogers's book are equally revealing. In 1908, a photograph of Will Rogers as a "prospective bridegroom" reveals a suave young gentleman who might have just walked out of a Wall Street brokerage; and one, no doubt, who appears to be capable of speaking grammatically correct Standard English. There is nothing, however, in this photograph to suggest that Will Rogers was country-born and raised. To the contrary, this Will Rogers appears to be a young man who is handsome, urbane, sophisticated, and extremely confident (102).

Another photograph of Will Rogers with his wife Betty in 1908, this one taken when he was "Sightseeing in Atlantic City," reveals a young man in his late twenties whose coat is buttoned and pulled up around his neck, and his hat is properly shaped and well-positioned on top of his head. In this photograph, Will Rogers is looking directly into the camera and smiling, but it is not the smile of the country buffoon or the noble rustic. It is, rather, a broad, almost handsome smile, probably precisely the kind of smile one would expect from a young man who was being photographed with the woman he loved (102).

In none of these early photographs do we detect the typical characteristics of the Oklahoma cowboy persona: chin lowered closer to the chest; head turned slightly off to the side; eyes twinkling good-naturedly and yet somehow mischievously, as they look up innocently at the viewer; hat pushed back on his head; and a whimsical smile spreading across his face. Nor is there even the hint or glimmer of the noble rustic or uneducated, semiliterate country buffoon lurking beneath the surface of this young man's personality. Until Will Rogers permanently adopted the persona of the Oklahoma cowboy, most observers would probably have to conclude that he appeared to be a handsome, reasonably sophisticated young man who could have been a successful business executive.

During Will Rogers's vaudeville experiences, which overlap with some of the above photographs, the Oklahoma cowboy persona begins to evolve into one of the warmest, most endearing stage personalities of the twentieth century. In an early vaudeville photograph of Rogers that appears in many sources, we can see the Oklahoma cowboy persona in its early stages of development (102). However, Will Rogers—although he is dressed in a cowboy hat, bandana, chaps, holster, and revolver—appears to be adopting the pose of the Hollywood film heroes, or the cowboy heroes of the dime novels, rather than the pose we have customarily come to associate with the working-class Oklahoma cowboy persona.

The face in this photograph is quite handsome, and it is accentuated by a slight, almost imperceptible grin. The eyes are open, but not truly focused on the viewer. The hat is pushed back on his head, but it is stylishly shaped and rounded. The bandana has been pressed and tied neatly around his neck. The carefully pressed dress shirt has impressive, large, white buttons on the sleeves and chest. His arms are holding a rope, but his hands are resting on his hips in a manner that almost projects a sense of youthful arrogance or cockiness. And the butt end of a revolver projecting out of his holster introduces a subtly threatening element into the photograph.

Although many of the props and stage symbols we associate with the Oklahoma cowboy persona are prominently displayed in the photograph, the metamorphosis is by no means complete. Furthermore, the total effect of the photograph creates the strongest impression that this slightly cocky cowboy rope artist feels he is somewhat superior to his surroundings—including his audience. The more mature Oklahoma cowboy persona will do everything in his power to assume the self-effacing pose of a man who considers himself to be of no great significance in the total scheme of things. Nor will he ever create the impression that he is superior to his audience. The earlier cowboy rope artist appears to be preoccupied with himself, whereas the more mature Oklahoma cowboy persona will subtly, almost shyly, deflect attention away from himself.

Another photograph that is reproduced in Betty Rogers's book, this one a 1913 photograph of Will Rogers when he had reached the apex of his career in vaudeville, reveals another stage in his gradual metamorphosis into the Oklahoma cowboy persona (52). Much of the paraphernalia and symbolism from the earlier vaudeville photograph are still evident, but the effect is much different. The 1913 vaudeville cowboy is dressed in leather chaps with his weight resting casually and informally mostly on one leg; arms somewhat shyly, almost defensively, folded across his body; his right hand holding a hat; eyes clearly focused on the camera; a rumpled bandana circling his neck; and the revolver and holster conspicuously absent. The cockiness and arrogance of the earlier vaudeville photograph are also nonexistent, replaced instead by the characteristic Rogers broad, good-natured smile spreading across his face as he looks out warmly at the audience (52).

In this photograph, Will Rogers has refined several aspects of the earlier vaudeville stage persona; or at least he has emphasized another side of his own personality. He has also mastered the body language and facial expressions of this character to create a much warmer, more engaging presence. Although the hat he holds is too stylish and neatly shaped, the shirt is too stylish, and the folded arms are perhaps a bit too defensive and self-contained for later versions of the Oklahoma cowboy persona, Will Rogers clearly understands this character. Although there is a difference in age, anyone who put this photograph next to other photographs of the handsome, carefully groomed man in a suit or sport coat would have to conclude that they are two different people. But they are not; one is Will Rogers, and the other is an emerging stage persona.

The Oklahoma cowboy persona will continue to evolve and become increasingly warm and inviting, yet simultaneously whimsical and playful. The working-class aspects of the Oklahoma cowboy will become increasingly simplified and the hat slightly more battered and shapeless. The lasso will be the most prominent stage prop, held loosely in a circular or oval shape to remind audiences of its working-class purposes, while simultaneously its role as a playful toy to be used and manipulated to delight audiences.

Over time, the exaggerated facial expressions Will Rogers developed for the silent movies enabled him to further refine this character. Nonetheless, the Oklahoma cowboy persona was obviously first developed in vaudeville and on the stages of the Ziegfeld Follies theater. The "Cherokee Kid," who performed rope tricks in Texas Jack's Wild West show, was undoubtedly the Oklahoma cowboy persona in embryo form. This persona is not the stereotypical poker-faced reporter or storyteller of the frontier tradition in American humor. The Oklahoma cowboy is much too warm, relaxed, and open with his audience to be labeled as simply another poker-faced reporter. Will Rogers, whose Oklahoma cowboy persona evolved out of the traditions established by the frontier humorists, virtually became the antithesis of the speakers in this tradition in this one very important respect. Unlike Sam Clemens, who molded his Mark Twain persona into the epitome of the poker-faced reporter and storyteller, Will Rogers instead created an open, warm, engaging, and good-natured stage and literary presence with the Oklahoma cowboy persona.

In some respects, it is difficult to compare the writings of Mark Twain and Will Rogers. Rogers himself spoke out against such comparisons. He acknowledged that Twain is in a class by himself as a writer and storyteller. He knew few, if any, writers would fare well in such a comparison. However, as Walter Isaacson points out in his book, *Ben Franklin An American Life*, the reason the Silence Dogood essays were so important is because "they were among the first examples of what would become a quintessential American genre of humor: the wry, homespun mix of folksy tales and pointed observations that was perfected by such Franklin descendants as Mark Twain and Will Rogers."[15]

These two descendants of Ben Franklin are also inseparably intertwined in the minds of the American people. This is especially true for older Americans. When we think of Will Rogers entertaining us with his rope tricks or in his films, we often think back to what we learned about Mark Twain earlier in our lives. They are like a pair of gifted humorists, one following the other in our imaginations.

Where yet another comparison can be made is that both men achieved the status of national icons, and they both used their power on a national stage. Without sacrificing their humor and resorting to preaching, they were champions of human decency and fairness in how we treat our fellow humans. This is especially true in Twain's efforts to expose the horrors of slavery through the slave Jim in *Adventures of Huckleberry Finn.* Jim is only trying to reunite his family, while the slave traders in the story have reduced humans to a commercial commodity to be bought and sold like cattle.

Will Rogers's role on our national stage was to be a spokesperson for *all* the poor and common people, but without alienating the wealthy and powerful. He was a champion of the less fortunate in systems that were often stacked against them. His fight was subtle, but his use of the electronic media made it equally effective.

As for the comparison between Will Rogers and Mark Twain regarding how they advanced our national consciousness through humor and laughter—it's a tie.

---

1. Albert Bigelow Paine writes in *Mark Twain, A Biography*, vol. 1 (New York: Harper and Brothers Publishers, 1912) that Sam Clemens's mother, Jane Clemens, was regarded as a "Kind-hearted, fearless . . . charitable, sympathetic woman . . . she joined the Presbyterian Church, and her religion was of that clean-cut, strenuous kind which regards as necessary institutions hell and Satan . . ." She was living proof that a humorist like Mark Twain could evolve out of a Puritan culture. Indeed, many of his jokes are directed at this rigid, doctrinal way of looking at life (35–36).
2. Will Rogers, *The Autobiography of Will Rogers* (Boston: Houghton Mifflin Company, 1949) 3–4.

3. Will Rogers, "How To Be Funny," *"How To Be Funny" & Other Writings of Will Rogers*, ed. Steven K. Gragert (Stillwater, Oklahoma: Oklahoma State University Press, 1983), 112–113.
4. Albert Bigelow Paine writes in *Mark Twain, a Biography*, vol. 3, that after Mark Twain died, "From every remote corner of the globe the cables of condolence swept in; every printed sheet in Christendom was filled with lavish tribute; pulpits forgot his heresies and paid him honor. No king ever died that received so rich a homage as his" (1579).
5. See Richard Ketchum's discussion of the reactions to Will Rogers's death in his book *Will Rogers, His Life and Times* 387–394.
6. The Will Rogers Library contains an impressive collection of the works of Mark Twain. Indeed, Mark Twain is the only "mainstream" American writer who is so fully represented in the library's holdings. The books by Twain are as follows: *Mark Twain* (volumes 1–23, with the exception of volume 9, which is missing); *The Adventures of Tom Sawyer*; *Mark Twain's Autobiography* (2 volumes); *A Connecticut Yankee in King Arthur's Court* (2 different editions); *Life on the Mississippi*; and *The Mysterious Stranger*. There is also a copy of W. R. Gillis's book *Gold Rush Days with Mark Twain* and other assorted books that make reference to Mark Twain both directly and indirectly. The copies of *A Connecticut Yankee in King Arthur's Court* appear to have been used by Will Rogers in preparing for his role as Hank Morgan in the film version of the novel. Just how much Will Rogers read or used any of the other books by Mark Twain is a matter of speculation. But it seems clear that he *did* use them, just as he used some of the other books in his library as occasional reference tools, if nothing else. Although he dismisses "book learning" as a way to acquire knowledge, Will Rogers certainly was not averse to filling in the gaps in his own knowledge of certain subjects by occasionally using his own personal library as a reference tool.
7. The Mark Twain aphorisms come from *Mark Twain's Greatest Witticisms and Sharpest Criticisms*, edited by B. Clay Shannon, and a variety of internet sources and public domain collections. The Will Rogers aphorisms come mostly from his newspaper columns, including: "Will Rogers Says," *San Francisco Chronicle*, July 03, 1932, 30; "Will Rogers Says Today," *San Diego Union and Daily Bee*, January 14, 1928; "Will Rogers Says Senate Is All Wind," *San Francisco Chronicle*, May 30, 1928; Will Rogers Says Today, *San Francisco Chronicle*, July 03, 1932; and other columns.
8. Public domain.
9. Mark Twain, *Adventures of Huckleberry Finn*, (Barnes and Noble: New York 2003) 5.
10. See Joel Chandler Harris's discussion of the importance of the oral storytelling tradition in the development of American literature in "From 'Humor in America' (1909), "*Critical Essays in American Humor*, eds. William Bedford Clark and W. Craig Turner (Boston: G. K. Hall & Co., 1984) 46–49.
11. *Cobblestone Magazine*, ed. Carolyn P. Yoder, vol. 5 num. 5, May 1984.
12. Gladys Carmen Bellamy, *Mark Twain as a Literary Artist* (Norman: University of Oklahoma Press 1950).

13. See Mark Twain's *Autobiography* 368–380.
14. Others like Spi Trent, author of *My Cousin Will Rogers*, remember Will as a warm, happy, carefree youth who evolved quite naturally into his role as the Oklahoma cowboy. However, when Homer Croy visited Will Rogers's birthplace to interview other people who had known young Will, he found that many of them did not speak very highly of their famous native son. Perhaps the only conclusion one can draw from this is that Will Rogers was indeed, as James M. Smallwood and Steven K. Gragert, editors of *Will Rogers Weekly Articles*, 6 Vols., 1980, have suggested, a man "who wore many hats."
15. Walter Isaacson, *Benjamin Franklin An American Life* (New York: Simon and Schuster Paperbacks, 2003) 29.

Will Rogers's birthplace (1879) in the Indian Territory in Oologah, Oklahoma. The frontier storytelling traditions he learned in his youth were instrumental in shaping his views of American humor. Betty Rogers, 1941. *Will Rogers, His Wife's Story*. Country Life Press Corp., N.Y.

Will Rogers (far right) on horseback with friends, including Lucille Mulhall (second from left) of Wild West Show fame (circa. 1900). For Will, horses and horseback riding were the symbols of freedom from civilized constraints even after he became a celebrity. The Gateway to Oklahoma History. Oklahoma Historical Society Photograph Collection.

Thomas Smith's *Self-Portrait* (1680) with a skull captures the Puritans' obsession with death, whereas public laughter was often viewed with suspicion. Somehow, America became a nation that celebrated humor even though it was discouraged in the early Puritan communities. Self-portrait of Smith, 1680. The York Project, 2002. Wikimedia.org. Public Domain.

Ben Franklin wears his fur cap to cover sores on his scalp, but also to bring a little levity and frontier humor to Europe. Wikimedia.org. Public Domain.

Mark Twain, America's foremost humorist and considered by many to be the "Lincoln of our literature," in a typical unsmiling, poker-faced expression. Twain's advice to other humorists was never let your audience know that what you have said or written is funny. *Adventures of Huckleberry Finn*, 1884. Harper Edition. Wikimedia.org. Public Domain.

Will Rogers posing shortly before his marriage to Betty. The contrast between the suave, handsome young man and his Oklahoma cowboy persona is striking. Betty Rogers, 1941. *Will Rogers, His Wife's Story*. Country Life Press Corp., N.Y.

Will and Betty posing for a photograph in Atlantic City in 1908. The well-dressed, handsome young couple look like they could have just stepped out of an exclusive downtown business or department store. Betty Rogers, 1941. *Will Rogers, His Wife's Story*. Country Life Press Corp., N.Y.

Will Rogers (1912) in his early glamorized garb modeled after film characters and western novels. Over time, he transformed this version of the Oklahoma cowboy into the more realistic working class, lasso-twirling, joke-telling persona. Wikimedia.org. Public Domain.

Will (c.1913) in a more relaxed, congenial Oklahoma cowboy pose. He gradually transforms the Oklahoma cowboy into a more inviting, warm and subtly whimsical version of this persona. Betty Rogers, 1941. *Will Rogers, His Wife's Story*. Country Life Press Corp., N.Y.

Will in a later version of the Oklahoma cowboy. Virtually all of the stage props have disappeared, except for the lasso, and he is dressed in more realistic, working-class garb, including a battered hat. Britannica Editors, 2025. *Will Rogers, American Humorist.*

The Rogers ranch-style home in Pacific Palisades, California. Will never stopped adding features that reminded him of his childhood home on the Oklahoma prairie. Santa Monica Public Library. Pacific Palisades Historical Society Digital Collection.

The interior of Will and Betty's home in Pacific Palisades, California. Like the exterior, the western-style décor of the interior enabled Will to escape into the memories of an earlier time in his life. Copyright and courtesy of California State Parks.

# VIII.

# LEGACY OF FRONTIER HUMOR

THERE ARE other ways Sam Clemens's "Mark Twain" and Will Rogers's "Oklahoma cowboy" persona are indebted to the traditions established by the frontier humorists. The Mark Twain persona is almost a refined synthesis or composite of virtually everything we associate with "the speaker" in traditional frontier humor. Some of this is due to Sam Clemens's own personal experiences on the frontier. Some of it is also due to his "stretching of the facts" so that this persona would fit into the characteristic satirical devices and identifiable traditions of frontier humor.[1]

Sam Clemens can honestly claim to have had little "formal education" because he had to go to work at the age of twelve to help support his family after the death of his father. Still, his satirical remarks regarding the inferior status of "book learning," and the superior status of "experience" as tools of knowledge, must nonetheless be taken with a grain of salt.[2] Twain certainly learned much from his own personal experiences as a riverboat pilot and gold prospector in the western mining territories.[3] But he was also intimately acquainted with the classics of world literature—including the plays of William Shakespeare, the Bible, the picaresque tradition in fiction, and the Arthurian legends—and he alluded to them frequently in his books and tales.[4]

In *Adventures of Huckleberry Finn*, Twain writes a humorous parody of Hamlet's "To be or not to be" soliloquy. The opening lines of Shakespeare's original soliloquy are:

> To be, or not to be? That is the question—
> Whether 'tis nobler in the mind to suffer
> The slings and arrows of outrageous fortune,

Or to take arms against a sea of troubles
And, by opposing, end them. To die, to sleep—
No more'—and by sleep to say we end
The heartache and the thousand natural shocks
That flesh is heir to . . .[5]

In Twain's novel, two frontier con artists try to find a way to impress the locals and make a few dollars by posing as Shakespearean actors. The openings lines of the soliloquy have been transformed as follows:

To be, or not to be; that is the bare bodkin
That makes calamity of so long life;
For who would fardels bear, till Birnam Wood
    do come to Dunsinane,
But that the fear of something after death
Murders the innocent sleep,
Great nature's second course,
And makes us rather sling the arrows of
    outrageous fortune
Than fly to others that we know not of time . . .[6]

Twain employs just about every element of frontier humor in his parody of the Shakespearean soliloquy. The King and the Duke are low-class characters who use vernacular speech patterns as substitutes for Shakespeare's beautifully phrased and poetic soliloquy. Their attempts to raise money through several schemes they concoct on the way down the Mississippi River with Huck explore the darker side, albeit humorously, of human nature. There is no poetry left in their soliloquy. There is just an oddball mixture of various lines from different Shakespearean plays, strung together in random associations that create the impression that the Duke and King are skilled actors, not the dregs of frontier society. However, to make these not-so-noble rustics believable and the parody work, Twain had to have an intimate knowledge of Shakespeare's plays.

Will Rogers also played the role of uneducated rustic, but he was obviously doing this to add a necessary dimension to his Oklahoma cowboy persona, and not because he was himself poor or uneducated.[7] As Peter

Rollins points out, Will Rogers may have been "an erratic student . . . [but] he had the equivalent of a high school education," which made him more educated than most Americans at that time in our nation's history (5). In spite of all the humorous and satirical comments Rogers directed at formal education, Richard M. Ketchum states that Rogers frequently "regretted not having taken advantage of the opportunities to acquire a good [college] education" (313). Although Rogers claimed, "I only know what I read in the newspapers," he, like Twain, was not simply an uninformed country bumpkin. Both men, even though they satirized book learning and formal education, went to great extremes to self-educate themselves in a variety of ways. However, since the frontier tradition of American humor required that the speaker be uneducated, both Mark Twain and Will Rogers stretched the facts to incorporate this personality trait into their respective stage and literary personae.

Sam Clemens, through the persona of Mark Twain, and Will Rogers, through the Oklahoma cowboy persona, also played the role of the "ugly" or "homely" American, as was expected of them as speakers in the traditions of frontier humor.[8] Twain's frequently caustic, satirical references to the aging process, especially as it affected his own physical appearance and state of mind, would by today's standards probably be condemned as "ageist" remarks. However, passing off oneself or an extended literary persona as "homely" or "ugly," and then using this strategy to justify comments about all types of human deformities, bodily functions, and various imperfections in human physiognomy was an acceptable satirical device in American frontier humor.[9]

Mark Twain's Huckleberry Finn's physical resemblance to a huckleberry that grows on a wild, uncultivated plant and his clothes covered with "grease and clay" qualify him as a "homely" or "ugly" American.[10] Once Mark Twain establishes these physically unappealing characteristics in his young narrator, he then allows Huck Finn to satirize all forms of human deformities and disabilities. The Widow Watson is described as "a tolerable slim old maid, with goggles on" (12). A drowned man who is found floating in the river is described as having been in the water so long "they couldn't make nothing out of the face . . . it warn't much like a face at all" (22). Pap is described as an animal in the form of a human being whose "hair was long and tangled and greasy and hung down, and you could see his eyes shining through like he was behind vines" (30).

Will Rogers also establishes his Oklahoma cowboy persona as an "ugly" or "homely" American for much the same reason; it is the most effective strategic and satirical position in frontier humor. However, many of the early photographs of Will Rogers reveal very clearly that he was neither homely nor ugly.[11] He was quite handsome, which, in addition to his sense of humor, accounts for the fact that he played "leading man" roles in many films.[12] Nonetheless, even his cousin Spi Trent plays into this tradition regarding the "homely" or "ugly" speaker when he comments, using his own form of frontier dialect, that Will wasn't much to look at when he was born:

> My folks are always Laffin about the way Will looked when he Entered This World . . . They tell about a bashful cow hand workin on the place who come in to look at the bundle of crinkled red flesh layin on his mamas knee, an how the cowboy just stood there scufflin his feet an tryin to find something nice to say an not bein able to (16).

In his autobiography, Will Rogers addresses this same theme when he comments on his own birth: "I was the youngest and last of 7 Children. My folks looked me over and instead of the usual drowning procedure, they said 'This thing has gone far enough, if they are going to look like this, we will stop'" (2). It is also clear from the photographs of the Oklahoma cowboy persona, during the time that Will Rogers was developing him in vaudeville, that Rogers gradually made this stage personality less and less physically attractive—even beyond what might be expected to occur during his own normal aging process. The early cowboy rope artist was a stage character whose physical appearance was so glamorized, almost romanticized, that he appeared to have just stepped out of a Hollywood film or the pages of a western novel (Ketchum, 102). Later, Rogers learned to accentuate the less attractive physical characteristics of this persona: the broad, almost corny grin that created a distinctively rustic look; the rumpled, shirt and bandana; and the battered hat (Ketchum, 2).

Once he established the Oklahoma cowboy as the "ugly" or "homely" speaker, Rogers then used this persona to satirize various human idiosyncrasies. However, his satire of human physiognomy is distinctively gentler than Mark Twain's more barbed, caustic descriptions. Rogers writes in "What a Woman Needs" that the major reason women haven't progressed as much as they would like in the twentieth century is because they spend too much time powdering their noses:

> That's what is holding women back nowadays. I tell you, when you take time out for powdering, the day is just about gone. It's getting so this country has two main occupations now. One is women pawing at their nose with a powder puff, and the other is the men talking about their golf scores (*Treasury*, 55).

In the same article, Will Rogers suggests that consistent powdering of their noses could result in permanent damage to women's faces: "Now, in the course of a couple of generations that will begin to tell on the race, and you will all have drooped mouth" (56). Will Rogers's humorous comments regarding women, although at times somewhat stereotypical, are gentler and less offensive than much of the satire that evolved out of the frontier tradition. In Rogers's article, women may "paw" at their noses, but there are no references to other physical defects or repulsive manners of behavior. They are also often described as stronger, wiser, and more resilient than men. (See chapter VI.)

Mark Twain respects no such proprieties. Women are as fair game as men. In "The Story of the Old Ram," he levels his satirical torch at some elderly women whose idiosyncratic behavior far exceeds anything Will Rogers would ever write. In this rambling tall tale, a slightly inebriated Jim Blaine tells a series of outrageous stories that have few connections except for the fact that they often describe the physical defects of several different characters. Blaine tells us that Miss Jefferson, an elderly woman, "had a glass eye and used to lend it to old Miss Wagner, that hadn't any, to receive company in; it warn't big enough, and when Miss Wagner wasn't noticing, it would get twisted around in the socket and look up, maybe, or out to one side." Miss Wagner also "borrowed Miss Higgins's wooden leg to stump around on; it was considerable shorter than her other pin . . . She said she couldn't abide crutches when she had company becuz they were so slow." These stories and a cavalcade of different characters go on for several pages, and then abruptly end when Jim Blaine falls asleep.[13]

There are no limits or boundaries to Mark Twain's humor. He frequently ridicules the victims of his satire, even women, as was typical of the frontier humorists. Will Rogers is normally more interested in poking gentle fun at people and their idiosyncrasies. The Oklahoma cowboy persona probably has more of Ben Franklin's Poor Richard in him, and he is more interested in teaching and informing than ridiculing. Not too many people would agree with newspaper columnist Ed Sullivan, who wrote a column on October 25, 1932, under the title "Celebrities." In this column, he compares the humor of Mark Twain and Will Rogers. Sullivan accuses Will Rogers of writing a humorous column that has "Too much bite and bitterness in his observations . . . [in which one] could smell flesh burning from a branding iron . . . [whereas] a fellow named Mark Twain . . . got laughs without sinking the barb."[14] Will Rogers was understandably hurt by Ed Sullivan's remarks, and he wrote back: "There is not a soul in public life that I 'got it in for' . . . Now, if I was, as you wrote, 'searing everybody with a hot branding iron,' I don't think I could have gone along this long. I couldn't hurt and insult everyone I meet and still last" (212).

Sam Clemens and Will Rogers are also extensions of the frontier tradition to the extent that they delight in playing the role of "originals," the cultural anomalies who seemingly sprang out of some remote chink far removed from mainstream American culture and history.[15] In part this cultural preoccupation with "original" characters and heroes can be traced all the way back to the earliest stages of American history, when an "original" nation was literally molded out of a wilderness. With such a background, it was probably inevitable that American culture, especially popular culture, would also celebrate those "original" folk heroes who seemed to spring up from some distant, seemingly unreachable corner of the New World.

Sam Clemens, as Mark Twain, played the role of the "original" for all it was worth. The pen name "Mark Twain" signifies "two fathoms" or "safe water" and is the leadsman's cry as he measures the depth of water from the bow of a steamboat. This pen name not only distanced Sam Clemens from the various literary personae he used in his stories and stage presentations. It also distanced him from his own ancestral roots. Once he assumed the pen name of "Mark Twain," Sam Clemens was no longer regarded by the public as an extension of the Clemens family history and ancestry. He was connected to the Mississippi River's history and mythology.

As Albert Bigelow Paine points out in *Mark Twain, A Biography*, after Sam Clemens died many Americans had disassociated him so much from his family tree that they preferred he should have been "laid to rest in the bed of that great [Mississippi] river which must always be associated with his name," rather than buried next to his wife and daughters (1580). Sam Clemens's use of this particular pen name was a masterstroke in creating the aura of the "original" that became the literary persona "Mark Twain."

Twain's manner of dress, especially later in life when he designed and wore his unique white suits, further enveloped him in the aura of the "original." These suits were unlike anything worn by his contemporaries except, perhaps, steamboat captains. Twain also referred to himself as "a freak of nature." He emphasized in his writings and stage appearances that he had been born in 1835, the year Halley's Comet was visible in the sky. He added that he planned to die when Halley's Comet returned in 1910—which he did (Bellamy 3). The impression Sam Clemens created with these repeated references to Halley's Comet was that he, or at least his Mark Twain persona, was indebted to some creative life force that existed in the Mississippi River, but also to an even greater force that existed in another world altogether. The aura of the "original" was thus complete. The subliminal message Sam Clemens sent out to the reading public was that "Mark Twain's" parents were not of human origins, but were rather the masculine and feminine forces inherent in Halley's Comet and the Mississippi River.

Will Rogers developed this cultural preoccupation with the "original" in his stage persona, but in a very different manner. Rather than creating a pen name that would distance him from his family history and ancestral tree, he recognized instead that his mixed white and Native American ancestry were themselves "unique" and "original." He chose to emphasize them in his Oklahoma cowboy persona. He was proud to point out that he was part Cherokee, and he admitted this probably accounted for some of his uniqueness.[16] He was equally proud of his Oklahoma heritage, especially the cowboy history he had experienced as a young boy and teenager. His Cherokee ancestry and Oklahoma cowboy roots would have been viewed by many Americans as truly "unique" or "original." Furthermore, his refusal to adopt a permanent stage name obfuscated the boundaries between Will Rogers and his Oklahoma cowboy persona, which is probably what he instinctively hoped to accomplish.

Will Rogers's western garb, when it was worn on stage in the middle of New York City several thousand miles from the original frontier, further enveloped him in the aura of the "original." His attempts to disguise the influences of both formal education and book learning on his own development as a humorist contributed greatly to the impression that the Oklahoma cowboy was an "original" of the type so admired by common, everyday Americans. However, as Donald Day points out in an introduction to Will Rogers's autobiography, the Oklahoma cowboy was not an "original." He was the product of a long historical and cultural tradition in America of authors, journalists, and storytellers who used pen names:

> Beginning in 1835 with Major Jack Downing until the death of Will Rogers, America was not without its cracker-box philosopher who often possessed power approaching or exceeding that of The President . . . Sut Lovingood, Artemus Ward, Petroleum V. Nasby, Bill Arp, Mark Twain, Josh Billings, M. Dooley—What an array (xiv)!

This is not to suggest that Sam Clemens and Will Rogers were imitating earlier frontier humorists. It is merely to suggest that they were not "new." Mark Twain was original to the extent that he took the elements he inherited from the frontier humorists and transformed them into art of the highest order. In the process, he created *Adventures of Huckleberry Finn* (1884), the national epic that had eluded the Hartford Wits in the eighteenth century. Will Rogers inherited many of these same elements from the frontier humorists, and he used them and his own personal experiences in the Midwestern territories to create a folk hero—the Oklahoma cowboy. Neither of these were small achievements. What Sam

Clemens and Will Rogers achieved ranks among the finest accomplishments of American culture. But they were not achieved in a historical or cultural vacuum. The cultural forces that shaped American humor demanded that the storyteller or literary persona be an original, even if it was a clever or instinctive pose.

The "moral visions" of Mark Twain and Will Rogers are also revealing in the context of M. Thomas Inge's comment that traditional frontier humor involved "a willing suspension of morality" (5). Whereas this may have been true of many of the original frontier humorists, it is not true of either Mark Twain or Will Rogers. Twain, in his own unique way, was very much an old-fashioned moralist, although he used the strategies of the humorist, rather than those of the preacher, to argue for certain moral standards.[17] The thematic focus of most of Twain's writings—with the exception of the later, more bitter works such as *Letters from the Earth,* not published until 1962, and *The Mysterious Stranger,* published in 1916—involve central characters who have a solid moral center. Even the protagonists in the more cynical literary works are not, in their bitterness, advocating a doctrine of amorality or immorality. They seem to be lamenting the fact that the human race appears to have lost its moral compass.

Huck Finn, Twain's most famous literary persona, is the most moral of characters even though he might not appear to be that way on the surface (Marx 328–329). Huck's gradual rejection of society's support for the institution of slavery, and his decision to help Jim escape to become a free man, are among the most poignant moral conflicts in our national literature. Through his humorous observations, Huck also promotes some simple virtues: common sense (Huck himself); compassion (for Jim, the duped Wilks family, and even the King and the Duke); charity (he willingly shares everything with Jim); and other such simple human virtues. Simultaneously, Huck satirizes virtually every human vice: drunkenness (Pap); greed and human exploitation (white racists, the King and Duke); hypocrisy (the Widows Watson and Douglas); and other such human failings.

Huck's apparent "idleness" is also more complicated. Although he loves to lie on the raft doing absolutely nothing while the river's current carries him downstream, he is often very busy and at times quite productive. Although he appears to be "self-indulgent," he is often more concerned about the welfare of others than he is for his own needs. He agonizes over the victims of the King and the Duke as they prey on unsuspecting, naive people during their journey down the Mississippi River. He also agonizes over Jim's predicament as an escaped slave.

Huck's major moral dilemma is that he has been conditioned by society to believe slavery is acceptable. However, during his adventures he gradually questions what he has been taught. At the end of the story, he is deeply troubled that his friend Tom Sawyer played a cruel joke on Jim rather than tell him that he had been freed in the Widow Watson's will.

In some ways, if Ben Franklin's Poor Richard was "roughed up" in terms of appearance and given a sense of humor, he might very well prove to be quite similar to Huck Finn. There is a simple wisdom and common sense that pervades their respective moral systems. One could argue that there is often a willing suspension of propriety and decorum in Twain's writings, but his stories frequently present the reader with a much higher moral code to emulate.

Behind the guise of the awkwardly grinning, semiliterate Oklahoma cowboy, Will Rogers is also in some ways an old-fashioned moralist, although this too does not appear to be the case on the surface. On stage, the Oklahoma cowboy appears to be an "idler," but he is really surrounded by the tools of his trade—rope, leather chaps, bandana, etc.—which connect him to the seemingly distant Puritan work ethic. Although Homer Croy points out that Will Rogers knew "many men he couldn't abide" (vii), the Oklahoma cowboy persona's comment, "I never knew a man I didn't like," even if it was taken out of context, implies that we should all try to be more "tolerant" of one another. Other old-fashioned virtues such as compassion, honesty, modesty, and humility are also promoted throughout his writings, while vices such as intolerance, pride, dishonesty, and greed are satirized.

Although the focus of Will Rogers's satire is to entertain audiences or readers, the moral center of what he presents on stage or in his writings is clear. Like some twentieth-century adult Huckleberry Finn, the Oklahoma cowboy persona uses humor to urge our government and political leaders to return to a simpler moral code, one governed by common sense, simple wisdom, and concern for the welfare of others.

Simultaneously, he satirizes greed, human exploitation, and the self-indulgent attitudes and policies of the wealthy upper classes. Like Mark Twain, he carries on the traditions of frontier humor, but he imbues them with a solid moral center.

Some of the "humorous strategies" Mark Twain and Will Rogers use in their respective writings offer a meaningful comparison. As Joel Chandler Harris argued in *The World's Wit and Humor* (1906), American humor evolved out of an *oral,* not a *literary* tradition. For that reason, the style of presentation, especially through the use of "what is frequently called dialect," is more important than subject matter (62). In his essay, "How to Tell a Story," Mark Twain makes a similar distinction when he writes: "The humorous story is American, the comic story is English, the witty story is French. The humorous story depends for its effect upon the *manner* of the telling; the comic story and the witty story upon the *matter.*" (216). For Twain, the word *manner* refers to virtually every aspect of storytelling style and strategies, but most importantly to the use of dialects, vernacular speech patterns, and idiomatic expressions. Critics and scholars have identified numerous dialects in his writings, each one accurately reproduced with painstaking precision.

In the essay, "How to Tell a Story," Twain lists several other strategies that are essential elements in humorous storytelling:

- The diversions in the humorous story are frequently more important than the story itself: "The humorous story may be spun out to great length, and may wander around as much as it pleases, and arrive nowhere in particular" (216).
- The punch line in the humorous story is often concealed or casually dismissed by the speaker: "The teller [of the story] will divert attention from that nub [punch line] by dropping it in a carefully casual and indifferent way, with the pretense that he does not know it is a nub" (216).
- The speaker must never drop the pose of the poker-faced storyteller: "The teller does his best to conceal the fact that he even suspects that there is anything funny about [the story]" (216).

- The humorous story frequently strings together exaggerations, incongruities, and absurdities into a comic mixture: "To string incongruities and absurdities together in a wandering and sometimes purposeless way, and seem innocently unaware that they are absurdities is the basis of the American art" (216).
- The storyteller must have a virtually infallible sense of timing and know how to use silence or pregnant pauses to generate laughter from the audience: "The pause is an exceedingly important feature in any kind of story, and a frequently recurring feature, too" (218).

When judged by these criteria, Will Rogers turns out to be a somewhat different, but equally effective writer and storyteller. He had a marvelous sense of comic timing. He knew how to use pauses and silence to generate laughter; and he could conceal or casually dismiss his punch lines without acknowledging that they were in any way significant. Will Rogers is not, however, the poker-faced reporter or storyteller. Nor is he, like Mark Twain, the master of numerous dialects and/or an expert in the humor of overstatement.

Rogers did experiment with different dialects and idiomatic expressions, and he had a keen ear for idiosyncratic speech patterns. However, he usually "roughs up" the language of his Oklahoma cowboy persona to approximate the dialect of average American working-class people. In his essay, "How to Be Funny," he uses Standard English as the basis for this dialect. Then he throws in grammatical mistakes, misspelled words, and awkward phrasing to recreate what his ear tells him is the language of common, everyday Americans speaking to one another:

> The interest they all show in it, you would think that all young America is practicing to be funny. I have tried to advise the Boys that I have known men in other walks of life that made more than comedians. But its just one of the things that you cant discourage anyone from, once they made up their minds. Its like these business men that go through life telling everybody they meet stories. The only novelty to it is that each man that tells it tells it worse than the fellow that just told you the same one down the Street (112).

Any high school English teacher or college professor could go through the above passage and identify numerous grammatical lapses that are variations from Standard English. Nonetheless, the foundation of Standard English is still very much evident beneath these grammatically incorrect colloquial expressions and vernacular styles of speech. Perhaps more importantly, these comments would not have worked if they were written in grammatically correct Standard English.

There were probably other reasons why Mark Twain wrote in many different dialects, whereas Will Rogers concentrated primarily on developing one universal American dialect with loosely defined grammatical standards. Mark Twain was writing at a time when the various regional and local dialects in this country had not yet coalesced into a more homogeneous form of American English. For him to attempt to establish such a universal language would have been to falsify the experiences he so accurately reproduced, something he satirically accused James Fenimore Cooper of doing in *The Leatherstocking Tales.* Mark Twain's writings not only reflect his intuitive gift for reproducing numerous dialects and vernacular speech patterns. They also reflect a nation of people with diverse ethnic and regional backgrounds and diverse ways of using the English language.

Will Rogers came upon the scene at a time when Americans were migrating to the cities in record numbers, thus creating both a more homogeneous population and a foundation for a more universally accepted form of American English. If Will Rogers had spoken or written in numerous dialects, he would never have found the one common voice that could reach this new audience. He would also have falsified the very experiences that provided the foundations for his stories and newspaper columns. He concentrated instead on mastering the one dialect he thought would appeal to the largest possible American audience. He had the dialect of the Oklahoma cowboy persona down perfectly, as is obvious by the way this stage personality was accepted by the American people.

Twain, as is clear from his essay, "How to Tell a Story," was also the master of *comic overstatement.* He was the master of other humorous styles as well, but he is extremely comfortable in the frontier tradition of the tall tale that utilized overstatement as its predominant satirical device.[18] Will Rogers, however, seldom uses comic overstatement on stage or in his writings. He is, instead, the master of *comic understatement*, which seems unusual when we consider the traditions of frontier humor out of which his Oklahoma cowboy persona evolved (Rollins 122–123). There are probably good reasons for this—reasons that demonstrate once again that he was no carbon copy of the frontier humorists. He had an intuitive gift for knowing what would or would not work on stage or in his writings. Fortunately, he allowed this intuition to guide him through the morass of less effective comic strategies. He had perhaps the most important tool for humorous writers: an uncanny ability to assess his audience and make whatever adjustments would be needed to reach them.

There is a final element in humorous writing that does not get as much attention as some of the other strategies. Walter Blair, in his book *Native American Humor* (1937), identifies three types of incongruity that are essential in humorous writing: incongruity between grammatical and ungrammatical forms of speech; incongruity between the time when the story is told, and the time when the story actually took place; and incongruity between the "realism" of the frame of the story, and the "fantasy" of the narrative itself (92).

There is probably one other incongruity that deserves mention in the context of Mark Twain and Will Rogers: the incongruity between the *demeanor* of the speaker, and the *manner* of style that is used in the actual telling of the story. Comic overstatement, for example, will usually not work with an overly expressive, demonstrative speaker because the incongruity between the demeanor of the speaker and the overstated manner of the storytelling style is lost. Similarly, comic understatement will usually not work with an undemonstrative, emotionally suppressed speaker for the same reason. The incongruity between the demeanor of the speaker and the understated storytelling style is also lost. There are exceptions, of course, but usually the principle of too much congruity between speaker and subject matter undermines many forms of humor.

Mark Twain, as the poker-faced reporter or storyteller, created considerable incongruity both on stage and in his writings when he was relating tall tales. For years, when actor Hal Holbrook recreated the Mark Twain persona on stage, audiences would roll in the aisles with laughter when he told the most outlandish, exaggerated tall tales in the solemn and apparently serious manner of the poker-faced reporter. Simultaneously, he would look up at the audience and act like he did not understand why they were laughing.

Similarly, Will Rogers created considerable incongruity on stage and in his writings when he adopted the more open, expressive manner of the Oklahoma cowboy persona, and yet had him relate stories using the classic traditions of comic understatement. When actor James Whitmore recreated the role of the Oklahoma cowboy persona on stage, he got numerous belly laughs when he deliberately understated a punch line. Then, through a gentle smile or sly grin, he revealed that it was a significant part of the monologue after all.

The art of storytelling, especially humorous storytelling, is almost always more skillfully rehearsed and practiced than the reader or stage audience suspects. The humorous storyteller who is writing or delivering the lines on stage must have impeccable control and timing. There is little room for error, even on a single word or syllable. Only a few actors or writers have perfected this intuitive sense of precisely how to deliver the right word and the right inflection to maximize their impact on the audience.

Mark Twain is rightfully held up as the master of this form of humor—and Will Rogers would not disagree. The argument can be made, however, that Rogers put just enough vernacular spin on the English language we had inherited from England to complete the transition into American English. He then adapted it first to the stage and later to radio and newspapers. His readers and listeners saw themselves in this humorous use of language precisely because he hadn't completely abandoned Standard English—their English—for humorous effect. He had given it just enough of a rhetorical twist so it would be funny to his audiences, but not so out of the reach of their understanding as to be incomprehensible. The verbal slips were a very important element in their language—perhaps even the most important element.

Twain's dialect and idiosyncratic speech patterns were masterstrokes of linguistic manipulation. He accurately replicated speech patterns created by race, education, literacy or lack thereof, and region or locale. Will Rogers created a linguistic lasso, and he used it with great skill to rope in the largest mass market audience of his time. That rope gradually encircled the country and eventually the world. It was a symbol of work transformed into play. It was a symbol of entrapment transformed into a symbol of liberation. It was a symbol of playful rebellion against a culture still laboring under an unrelenting, inherited work ethic. It spoke in its own language in silent words that were felt more deeply than spoken words.

Perhaps most importantly, the lasso was a symbol of hope that grew and became more expansive the longer it was twirled. It grew in size until it encircled everyone, creating a single show of humanity that reveled in the joy of its unifying presence.

---

1. Justin Kaplan, *Mr. Clemens and Mark Twain* (New York: Simon and Schuster, 1966) 30–31.
2. Gladys Carmen Bellamy, in her book, *Mark Twain as a Literary Artist* (Norman: University of Oklahoma Press 1950), very perceptively points out that Mark Twain's "light-handed attitude towards his own literary work . . . must always be taken with a grain of salt, just as his disparagement of his own knowledge of books must be" (34). Similarly, Minnie M. Brashear, in her book *Mark Twain, Son of Missouri* (Chapel Hill: University of North Carolina Press, 1934) points out that Mark Twain's denial of the importance of book learning in his own development "was a part of the legend he deliberately created about himself, either because it pleased his vanity to believe that what he had read had been of small value in his development, or because he knew that he was more interesting to his American public in the role of an original than as a man who had from boyhood extended his powers . . . by diligent reading. He was unacademic, but not unliterary." Brashear concludes that Mark Twain's readings were so extensive that he "became a . . . critic of the best in literature by the time he was twenty-five years old."
3. See Mark Twain's *Roughing It* (1872) and *Life on the Mississippi* (1883).
4. *Adventures of Huckleberry Finn* has a picaresque structure similar to that employed in Henry Fielding's *Joseph Andrews*, Cervantes's *Don Quixote*, and other such classics of world literature. Twain's detailed knowledge of the Bible is evident in his characterizations of the Widows Watson and Douglas. And he certainly knew enough Shakespeare to do a marvelous job of parodying Shakespearean blank verse as it is performed by the characters of the King and the Duke in the same novel.
5. William Shakespeare, *Hamlet*, ed. Jeff Solven, Barnes and Noble: New York (2007) 189–190.
6. Mark Twain, *Adventures of Huckleberry Finn*, Barnes and Noble: New York (2003) 125.
7. The fact that Will Rogers had a library, and that he used it occasionally is evidence in itself that he was, if not an avid reader, at least a man who recognized the value of books and used them when necessary. Just how much Will Rogers used this library

is a matter of speculation. But the underlining, marginal notations, and occasional worn bindings indicate that he did use them. This casts great suspicion on his statement that "All I know is what I read in the papers." This statement seems, instead, to reflect a necessary element in his Oklahoma cowboy persona, rather than a valid statement about his own personal life and reading activities.

8. See Jennette Tandy's article, "An American Comic Character" 1925.
9. See Milton Rickels's article, "The Grotesque Body of Southwestern Humor" (1984).
10. Mark Twain, *Adventures of Huckleberry Finn* (New York: The Bobbs-Merrill Company, Inc., 1967) 21.
11. See especially the photographs that are reproduced in Betty Rogers's book, *Will Rogers, His Wife's Story* (1941), and Richard M. Ketchum's book, *Will Rogers, His Life and Times* (1973).
12. See the photographs that are reproduced in Bryan B. and Frances N. Sterling's book, *Will Rogers in Hollywood* (1984).
13. Mark Twain, "The Story of the Old Ram," *Major Writers of America*, Vol. II, (Harcourt, Brace and World, 1962) 72–74.
14. Ed Sullivan, "Celebrities," in Bryan B. and Frances N. Sterling's book, *Will Rogers World* (New York: M. Evans and Company, 1989) 211.
15. See the discussion of the concept of the "original speaker" in frontier humor in Minnie M. Brashear's *Mark Twain, Son of Missouri* (Chapel Hill: University of North Carolina Press, 1934).
16. See the discussion of Will Rogers's ancestry, and especially his Cherokee heritage, in Richard M. Ketchum's book *Will Rogers, His Life and Times* (New York: McGraw-Hill Company, 1973) 21–26.
17. See the chapter titled "Mark Twain's Religion" in Albert Bigelow Paine's *Mark Twain, a Biography*, vol. 3 (New York: Harper and Brothers Publishers, 1912) 1581–1585. Paine argues most convincingly that although Mark Twain was somewhat scornful of most religions because his own "religion was a faith too wide for doctrines," he was nonetheless a most moral man and author, for he "strove against oppression, shame, and evil in every form" (1584).
18. James M. Cox, *Mark Twain, The Fate of Humor* (Princeton: Princeton University Press, 1966) 96–103.

# IX.

# SEARCH FOR A NEW FRONTIER

ALTHOUGH MARK Twain and Will Rogers were both products of the frontier tradition in American humor, they extended that tradition in two slightly different directions in terms of their satirical and humorous styles. However, their relationship to the American frontier is not restricted exclusively to frontier humor. Rather, a sense of opening and closing frontiers pervades their respective lives, careers, and literary personae.

Both Sam Clemens and Will Rogers adopted several other stage and literary personae in their respective lifetimes. Sam Clemens wrote under the pen names of "Josh" and "Thomas Jefferson Snodgrass," as well as "Mark Twain."[1] Will Rogers performed under the stage names of the "Cherokee Kid" and "Jubilo," but only the "Oklahoma cowboy" persona, and its mature version in the form of the "statesman-philosopher," left a lasting impression on the American public. The Cherokee Kid had mastered all the necessary western rope tricks, but he did not tell stories.[2] Jubilo, although he was an extension of American comic types that go all the way back to Ben Franklin, was ultimately too much the clown to be associated with frontier culture and history.[3]

Only the Oklahoma cowboy, like Sam Clemens's Mark Twain, was able to achieve the status of mythical folk hero and cultural icon in the hearts of the American people. Perhaps this says as much about America as it does about Will Rogers and Sam Clemens. The mystique of the frontier and its place in American history and mythology may partially account for the fame they achieved.[4] They were identified so closely with the American frontier as to be inseparable from that time in our nation's history—the time when it was still possible to find the escape valve in the West.

Mark Twain and Will Rogers were both "escape artists" who evolved out of the frontier phase in American history. Twain, who had direct experience with the California Gold Rush, which he chronicled in *Roughing It* (1872), spent a good part of his life thereafter obsessively traveling to various parts of the planet trying to recapture the excitement of the original American frontier experience. In his early works, such as *The Innocents Abroad* (1869), we sense an optimism that is based on his faith in the resiliency of the American spirit and character. In his later work, *Adventures of Huckleberry Finn* (1884), the reader senses his (and Huck's) growing awareness that the American frontier is closing. At the end of the novel, Huck laments the civilized world that has entrapped him: "I reckon I got to light out for the territory ahead of the rest, because Aunt Sally she's going to adopt me and sivilize me, and I can't stand it. I been there before (264)." With that parting statement, Huck articulates the feelings of many Americans. They, too, were losing their escape valve in the West that promised so much, and yet frequently demanded such exorbitant personal sacrifices as the price to be paid for those promises.

For much of his life, Twain set out to do something that hundreds and thousands of Americans would try to do throughout the next century. He tried to create a new escape valve for himself and his literary characters. Ultimately, Twain recognized that there was no escape—not from time, mortality, or any of the boundaries that gradually surround and entrap the human spirit. Whereas the case for Twain's eventual pessimism has probably been somewhat overstated, there can be no question that his personal losses, together with the closing of the escape valve in the West, contributed significantly to his growing sense of the futility of human life. Perhaps nothing in American literature is more ironic and painfully tragic than the fact that Mark Twain, who created Huckleberry Finn, one of the most individualistic spirits in all of world literature, wanted only one thing at the end of his life, and that was to be a part of a family.[5]

Unlike Twain, who outlived his wife and two daughters, Will Rogers died before any of the other members of his family (Ketchum 166–167).

He never had to experience the loneliness and despair that Twain endured while he sat virtually alone, in a huge empty house in Connecticut, while the body of his beloved daughter Jean lay on a bed in a nearby bedroom.

Will Rogers was never to know that loneliness and despair. Toward the end of his life, he did become more aware of the painful realities that encrusted the spirit and entrapped the human soul (Croy 274–292). Escape artist that he was, he became a wandering reporter, unofficial American ambassador to various foreign countries, and finally the lone passenger on Wiley Post's airplane as they headed out for yet another last frontier in Point Barrow, Alaska.

Even as he watched frontier after frontier closing behind him, Will Rogers seemed to preserve in his spirit something of the buoyant optimism that had sustained those pioneers who had participated in the original westward movement. He insisted on building his home in Pacific Palisades in the ranch house style of his youth, and not the Spanish revival style his wife Betty preferred. When Betty brought home plans for the Spanish revival style drawn by a well-known architect, Will voted against them. He wanted the ranch house to be the place where he was surrounded by some of the memories from his earlier life on the Oklahoma prairie. Subsequent additions to the house were designed to complement the same ranch style.[6]

The ranch house and its evolving design became an obsession for Will. In his mind it was never completed. It always needed additions and modifications. It became a reflection of the restless, wandering spirit he had experienced in his youth and for much of his life. Betty wrote in her book, "If Will had a free day, he liked to hop in a car and drive off without any plans. He would call to me, 'Come on, Blake; let's get going,' and away we'd go . . . To get off the highway on a strange dirt road was what Will liked best" (272–273).

The ranch house was a comforting presence in his life, but real frontiers were becoming more difficult to find. For a spirit that sought always to look ahead with hope and optimism, the escape valves were beginning to appear more tantalizing somewhere in the earlier years of the nation's history. He did not show any signs that he would eventually become a misanthrope, as was the case with Twain. That would be most uncharacteristic of him. Still, he no doubt was finding it more difficult to unbridle his spirit as he had unbridled his pony to let it run freely across the Indian Territories, when that remote area of land was still part of the original American frontier.

For Will, horses were as important as family members. When they were building the ranch home in Pacific Palisades, he wanted a plan that would enable his family and friends to "ride our horses and hitch em right in front of the house."[7] He designed the study where he did much of his writing near "a large window next to [his] desk that looked out on the barn and the hills where horses grazed." If the view got too tempting, he could climb down a special "sneak stairway" that got him outdoors without encountering any guests who might have stopped by (Yagoda, 270). Sometimes, after he snuck out of the house, he would go over to the barn to be with the horses. At other times, he would go for a ride to free his mind.

To Will, horses were more than animals he kept in the stables of his Pacific Palisades ranch and took out occasionally for a ride. They were symbols of freedom, especially the freedom of the Indian Territories he had ridden across in his youth. In many ways, he saw horses as superior to the humans who rode them. Horses did not start wars. They did not kill anyone, at least not intentionally. And they seemed happiest when they were running across a Midwestern prairie, the wind flowing through their manes and seemingly merging with the life force of nature itself.

Will enjoyed some escapes from his celebrity status while riding on the ranch with the Los Angeles city skylight stretching into the clouds in the distance. But his Pacific Palisades ranch was not the Oklahoma prairie. It provided a brief, albeit immeasurably valuable, self-sustaining memory of the freedoms he hungered for even as he rode to fame in a country and culture his Cherokee ancestors had fought against and later joined.

We can only ponder what he must have felt during his last years living in a country that enabled him to become one of the most admired people of his time. The prairie he grew up on was so empty. Yet, it was still free and unencumbered. Did he ever long to be back there and away from the fame that was so fulfilling, yet entrapped him in other ways?

Yes, some of this is speculation. Yet, that restless, wandering presence lingered over the ranch even long after he was gone.

In the early 1930s, Will was asked to visit China and Japan as "an observer of war conditions." He was aware of the military build-ups that would inevitably lead to World War II, but he appeared to be uncertain as to what he was supposed to look for on that trip. At a stopover in Medford, Oregon, he joked about the reasons why he was being asked to visit the two countries: "I have no idea why I am going to Japan, and wish somebody would tell me. The trip will take 11 days, and I'll be seasick ten of them. I can't talk Japanese—just barely get by with my own language. The Japs don't like wisecracking. I'm not going to mess with them. They are going to hear the awfullest lot of compliments they ever listened to."[8] Behind the wisecracks and humor, one senses in his writings that he was aware of the build-up of the war machine in Japan, and he knew what it portended for the entire world. Still, he did not drop the identity of the slightly baffled, somewhat ignorant persona that had served him so well on stage, films, and newspaper columns.

Perhaps it is not stretching the point to say that of all the literary personae developed by nineteenth- and early twentieth-century American humorists and satirists, there are only two that can be described as truly brilliant: Sam Clemens's *Mark Twain* and Will Rogers's *Oklahoma cowboy*. These two personae, the products of both art and craftsmanship, were drawn from the deepest wellsprings of American culture and offered to the American people so naturally and apparently effortlessly as to seem real. But they were not real. Or rather they were more real than they could ever have been if they had truly existed. They transcended reality and became rugged, earthy, stage fantasies conjured up from both myth and history by two master artist-magicians.

To deny that Mark Twain is Sam Clemens's literary persona would be to deny him his greatest accomplishment. Mark Twain still walks the stages of our memories, smoking long cigars and telling tall tales long after Sam Clemens, his creator, has ceased walking the lonely corridors of his Connecticut home, reminiscing about his lost family.

So it is with Will Rogers. We do his memory a disservice if we grant him anything less than his rightful due—and that is to acknowledge he was not only a first-rate humorist. He was also an extraordinarily talented artist. So talented, in fact, that although he died in a tragic airplane crash in 1935, his Oklahoma cowboy persona still performs rope tricks and walks the invisible stages in the collective memories of the American people.

---

1. See Walter Blair, *Native American Humor* 560–561.
2. See Ketchum (74–75) and Rollins (162).
3. See Sterlings, *Will Rogers in Hollywood* 20–21.
4. Although John Wayne had leading roles in many different film genres, he achieved a special, almost legendary status in the eyes of the American people primarily because he became so closely identified with the frontier in films such as *Stagecoach, The Searchers, The Alamo*, and other movies about the West. Clint Eastwood is another actor whose lasting fame is probably due more to his roles in westerns than his roles in other film genres.
5. See Mark Twain's *Autobiography* 371–380.
6. California State Parks' microfilmed documents illustrate the preferred architectural styles during the construction of the ranch house in Pacific Palisades.
7. Ben Yagoda, *Will Rogers, A Biography* (University of Oklahoma Press, 1993) 266.
8. *The Medford Mail Tribune*, November 20, 1931, 1. Rev. by Ben Truwe and republished in *Southern Oregon History*, May 29, 2025.

# X.

# CULTURAL ICON AND HUMANITARIAN

TO MANY Americans, the name "Will Rogers" immediately creates an image of the Oklahoma cowboy on stage twirling his rope and encouraging it to do tricks no rope should be able to do. That's how most of us, especially older Americans, remember him. In our minds, he is connected to the West and an earlier time when the prairie territories had only recently become states. Somehow that image we have of him escapes the ravages of time. He stands alone, the symbol of a bygone era that never faded completely into the shadows of history.

Many Americans are not aware that Will Rogers had other careers in addition to his Oklahoma cowboy persona. The Oklahoma cowboy was such a strong symbol of rural frontier America that it subsumed the other aspects of his life. However, its creator Will Rogers achieved national and international fame long after his stage performances, movies, and other forms of entertainment he engaged in had faded.

His journalism career was especially important in shaping his life. He wrote a syndicated column under the title "Will Rogers Says" for *The New York Times* from 1922–1935. The column reached some forty million readers and helped him become a household name—if he wasn't already one.

His columns brought homespun rural humor to the cities and the nation as a whole. One column, written for the *Evening Vanguard* (September 3, 1925), was reminiscent of the frontier storytellers who would describe a local character playing a practical joke on an outsider, usually someone from a big city. In this column, Rogers plays the role of the narrator and outsider: "At the crossroads I asked the farmer, 'Where does this road go?' Says he: 'It don't go nowhere. It's always been here."[1]

Another column in the *South Gate Press* (July 10, 1931) satirizes the modern propensity to "overpredict" where the future might be taking us: "Will Rogers says what this country is suffering from is over-prediction. Predicting with both knees under a well-loaded banquet table is America's favorite indoor sport."[2]

Some of his columns, like one that appeared in *The Sacramento Union* (January 8, 1934), address more serious issues, including threats of war and nations that are covetous of other nations' lands and resources. Even though these were serious threats in Rogers's own time, he tends to write them in the same laid-back, commonsensical, understated tone and style that might be used to describe two rural farmers trying to negotiate a minor boundary dispute involving their adjacent cornfields or wheat fields: "This thing of living in an ambitious nation is not what it's cracked up to be. We are certainly glad Roosevelt announced that we had all the country we wanted."[3]

Rogers's job as a journalist also provided the opportunity for him to wander everywhere and anywhere. Like many others who were born in the last decades of the nineteenth century, he inherited the restless, wandering spirit of the previous generation. The difference was the earlier generation went in search of gold or land or whatever dreams they saw on the western horizon, and they set off in that direction. Rogers's wanderings took him just about anywhere that appealed to him at the moment, or anywhere he saw that his presence might do some good.

During his lifetime, Rogers understood the threat Hitler's Germany posed to the world. He had lived through World War I and knew of the slaughter that occurred on those European battlefields. He was mostly a pacifist who thought America should avoid foreign entanglements and wars whenever possible. But he was also a deeply empathetic man who used his fame to help the world's poor and suffering.

In the far more complex world after his death, we cannot help but wonder how his homespun humor, light satire, and gentle rebukes of the world's political leaders would have played out had he lived into the 1940s. Would his gentler satirical approach still work in a world torn apart by atrocities on an epic scale, cities littered with decaying corpses killed during aerial bombings, and entire races of people executed or allowed to slowly waste away in concentration camps? He certainly did not see all of this coming. How could he?

What we do know is he was a humanitarian throughout his life. Hunger and poverty were no longer jokes in a stage monologue. They were everyday challenges for a large percentage of the human population. He saw those things and they bothered him deeply.

In time, he became even more involved in efforts to relieve the sufferings of the nation's poor and hungry. During the depths of the Great Depression, angered by Washington's inability to feed the people, he embarked on a cross-country tour for the Red Cross. His own successes and good fortunes in life never blinded him to those who lived every day not knowing where they would sleep, or where they would find their next meal.

His commitment to humanitarian concerns was so deep that the National Society of Newspaper Columnists in 1999 created an award in his honor. The Will Rogers Humanitarian Award is presented yearly to the newspaper columnist "whose work has positively affected readers' lives and produced humanitarian benefits." The description of the award also notes that Rogers "was a great humanitarian, helping many worthwhile causes and giving much of his fortune to charities. He used his public forum to raise millions of dollars for victims of floods in the South, drought in the Southwest, and earthquakes in Latin America. Leading a Red Cross national relief tour during the Great Depression in 1931, he stirred communities to action."[4] He also used his celebrity status to support efforts to ease the human suffering caused by worldwide epidemics and natural catastrophes.

After Rogers's death, his wife Betty carried on the tradition: "During World War II, she gave ranch tours to benefit the Red Cross and the Salvation Army. Before she died in 1944, she arranged for the property to be deeded to the State of California for inclusion in the state park system as a commemorative tribute to her late husband." The one stipulation in the deed was that the ranch be kept open to local polo players to be used as their playing field. Betty, like her husband, was committed to building bridges between people of different social classes. They were always aware that others were not as fortunate in life. Their fame did not cause them to think of themselves as anything more than "just common folks," to use the language of Will's rural Oklahoma ancestors.[5]

Will Rogers never gave up on humanity. He always believed the good in human nature was stronger than the evil. He looked for the best in everyone. Would an increasingly violent world in the next decade have changed that?

During the times he was back in his ranch home, we can only speculate on how he viewed the world from his secluded oasis away from the turmoil he witnessed during his travels. On his ranch, he was surrounded by western-style furniture, his library of mostly western novels, and the horse stables and barns. Most of all, he had a little open land in Pacific Palisades that was not in any way commensurate with the Oklahoma prairie where he had spent his youth—but it was the closest thing to a ranch on the edge of a big city.

Homer Croy wrote that Rogers, in the months before his death, was "increasingly careless about his writing," as though he simply had neither the energy nor the desire to maintain his public persona. Reflecting on Rogers's apparent need to remain more and more in touch with his private self, Croy also writes that Rogers "was filling fewer lecture engagements; it was more fun to ride over the ranch" (293).

The escape valve in the West had closed almost half a century earlier. Civilization had won. The original frontier was gone. It left behind people like Will Rogers who longed for a frontier after the original frontier was only a memory. Maybe he felt he had outlived his time. Maybe he felt the only option was to keep moving. In some respects, he was one of the most common characters in our national literature—the wanderer without any destination.

When Will became deeply involved in humanitarian concerns, they satisfied his instinctive need to wander. This is not to suggest those concerns were anything other than his deeply felt empathy for the majority of the world's population who struggled every day merely to survive. It is to suggest that he, like all wanderers, needed to wander to feel alive and to experience life to the fullest, even as he was fulfilling his deeply felt commitments to the rest of humanity so they could share the fruits of his fame.

---

1. *Evening Vanguard*, Sept. 3, 1925.
2. *South Gate Press*, July 10, 1931.
3. *The Sacramento Union*, January 8, 1934.
4. The Will Rogers Humanitarian Award was created in 1999 by the National Society of Newspaper Columnists to honor journalists who follow Rogers's example that "journalism has an obligation to public life—an obligation that goes beyond just telling the news or unloading lots of facts."
5. Will Rogers State Park Microfilm Collection.

# XI.

# SIFTING THROUGH THE RUINS

IN THE days and weeks after January 7, 2025, I continued to follow the events in Pacific Palisades where the wildfires had roared out of control and destroyed almost every structure in their paths. I hoped that some of the structures in the Will Rogers State Historic Park could somehow avoid the devastation. Later that month a television reporter on the scene reported that, except for a ranger station, the buildings and almost everything in them had been destroyed. The chairs where Will Rogers had sat, and the tables where he had eaten or played cards—they were all gone. No one would ever again have the experiences I had over thirty years earlier, when I sat in those chairs and paged through those books and felt his presence everywhere in his ranch home.

I felt a few moments of gratitude that I was able to see and use those documents and historical records before they were destroyed. Those feelings did not last for long. They were followed almost immediately by a deeper sadness that much of the legacy of Will Rogers, a man who had filled this country with so much hope and human decency, was gone—vanished forever.

I hoped some of the memories of that legacy would live on in the Will Rogers Memorial Museum in Claremore, Oklahoma, and the restored Rogers family home also in Oklahoma. Still, the loss of the ranch home and other structures in Pacific Palisades was immeasurable.

I decided, after viewing the destruction on television and locating my earlier manuscript, I needed to resurrect that project and somehow bring it to completion. I needed to return to the question I had asked myself when I sat in his library many years earlier: *Who was Will Rogers, and why did he mean so much to this nation?*

I soon realized the answer to that question was ultimately not in the rubble that was once his home. It was in the values of the nation he had helped to shape, a nation that never gave up hope in its darkest hours, a nation that at its best encouraged all Americans to work together to defeat a common enemy or achieve the common good. No, it was never perfect. But we seemed to be able to rise to the occasion so many times before when a national or worldwide threat rose again from the darkest side of human nature.

As I searched through my notes that had yellowed with age, I found some scribbled comments I had written down thirty years earlier. I tried to reconstruct in my mind the day Will Rogers died, and the reaction of an entire nation to his death in the weeks and months that followed. On August 15, 1935, the news from Point Barrow regarding the death of America's favorite son slowly trickled out of that remote part of Alaska. People were glued to their radios. All that was really known was Will Rogers had died, along with his friend and pilot, Wiley Post. Everyone wanted to know the details of how it had happened. Eventually, witnesses described how the plane carrying both men had struggled to gain altitude. Soon there was a sputtering sound coming from the engine. Then the sputtering sound stopped. For a few precious moments, all was quiet. Then the plane quickly fell out of the sky and crashed into the Alaskan tundra.

My wife Alexa offered to help me find some newspaper accounts of Will Rogers's death, so I could verify my own memories of what I had read in the early 1990s. She came back with several headlines and obituaries, most of them written the next day, August 16, 1935, after the tragic accident. The enormity of the loss to the nation and the world practically screamed in anguish from the headlines of the newspapers.

*The Longview Daily News* (August 16, 1935) in Longview, Texas, published several articles under the headline written in capital letters and covering virtually the entire front page: "WILL ROGERS AND WILEY POST KILLED IN AIRPLANE TRAGEDY." The subtitle, also in capital letters, read "LONGVIEW MOURNS DEATH OF PAIR." Another article on the same front page, titled "TRAGEDY SHOCKS PRESIDENT, MANY MILLIONS PEOPLE," provided some of the details regarding eyewitness reports of how the plane went down.[1]

*The Evansville Press* (August 16, 2035) in Evansville, Indiana, published an article under the headline, again in capital letters, "WILL ROGERS AND WILEY POST ARE KILLED IN AIRPLANE CRASH." Virtually the entire front page was filled with other articles regarding the crash and the lives of Will Rogers and Wiley Post. One of the articles was titled "Death Ends Quips That Made Millions Laugh," acknowledging that Rogers's death was not only a great loss to the nation, but also to the entire world.[2]

*The Daily Ardmoreite* (August 16, 1935) in Ardmore, Oklahoma, introduced its front page coverage of the tragedy with the title, "WILL ROGERS AND POST KILLED." A brief caption above a photograph of Rogers indicated, "Nation Weeps to Learn of Will Rogers' Untimely Death in Crash." A subsequent article under the title, "CLAREMORE CLOSES DOWN," described how the entire population of Claremore shut down their businesses so people could spill out into the streets and share their grief. Another article in the same newspaper quoted one mourner who said, "He was a good man with a wealth of common hard sense that made him an international figure. It is the greatest loss Claremore ever had." Coverage of Rogers's death swept every other news article of the day into the back pages of the newspaper.[3]

The *New York Daily News* (August 17, 1935) covered the tragedy under the headline, "FROM COWBOY TO FILM IDOL, ROGERS LIFE." The coverage of Rogers's death again covered virtually the entire front page. A short accompanying article stated, "Death of Will Rogers and Wiley Post created a widespread reaction here today. In streets, subways, shops and thousands of homes the tragic crash in Alaska was the chief topic of conversation." The front page coverage also indicated that the grief the nation felt over the loss of its favorite humorist was so intense, "stocks dropped from 16 ¾ to 15 ½." An article on the same page indicated, "All of world sees loss in air tragedy."[4]

Similar headlines and articles appeared in newspapers all across the country and overseas. The loss was felt everywhere. The Oklahoma cowboy who had brought so much joy and laughter, even into the early years of the Great Depression, was gone. Throughout the nation, and in many other parts of the world, Will Rogers's death brought businesses and normal daily activities to a temporary halt. The grief was so profound that it seemed everyone had taken notice of the loss of someone they had grown to love and admire, even though they had known him mostly through his films, radio broadcasts, and newspaper columns.

People everywhere were asking the same questions: How do you mourn such a loss? How do you replace a favorite son who had endeared himself so deeply into our national consciousness? How do you ease the pain of that loss?

The answer to that question was inevitable. You don't replace it. You can only gather up as many fragments of it that might still be scattered around the parts of the world he had visited or the people he had touched.

While I was trying to comprehend the enormity of the deeply felt reactions to Will Rogers's death, Alexa handed me a photocopy of something else she had researched. It was a form titled "Cherokee Nation. Cherokee Roll," which appeared to be a registry for people who wished to be officially enrolled in the "Cherokee Nation" if they met the qualifications criteria. An accompanying description stated, "Rogers's application to the Dawes Commission in 1900 was accepted, and he was enrolled as a member of the Cherokee Nation." On the lines below the description, the handwritten names of Will's father, "Clement," and his own first name, "William," were entered. His middle name, "Penn Adair," was also entered in the spaces provided. That name, as I soon learned, was the name of a former Cherokee leader "Colonel William Penn Adair."[5]

The fact that Will was twenty years old when he filled out the application seemed significant. He was not just a child whose father signed his name on the form. He was old enough that his permission would probably have been needed. His decision to allow his father to enroll him as a member of the "Cherokee Nation" must have reflected the pride he felt in his own Cherokee heritage. Will Rogers always considered himself to be both an American and a Cherokee. He was clearly proud of his bloodlines that could be traced back to some of the earliest inhabitants of this continent.

A more recent article, titled "Will Rogers was always a Cherokee" and published by *Indian Country Today*, verifies that he always had a deep and personal relationship to his Native American heritage. The article, written by Vincent Schilling and published in 2020, states, "No matter how popular he was, Will Rogers was always a Cherokee . . . He reminded people every day that there are native people of this land still alive and who remain a vibrant part of America's tapestry."[6]

I soon realized my book, *Will Rogers Storyteller*, should refer not only to the stories he told on stage or in films. It should also refer to his own life's journey, which was in many ways the most remarkable of his stories. Born into the Oklahoma Indian Territory, where his Cherokee heritage was a major part of his life story, he entered adulthood when Native Americans were often portrayed in films as the villains. They were the savages covered in war paint attacking wagon trains, families, or individuals traveling through their lands. Film audiences became accustomed to these fierce warriors hiding in the mountains, in wilderness areas, or concealed in the rolling hills of the prairie lands, waiting to pounce on white settlers spreading into territories Native Americans had lived for centuries. Will's gentle satire and charitable heart, reflected in his humanitarian activities throughout his life, helped force this nation to overcome these stereotypes.

Will had much in common with Sitting Bull, who tried to avoid the massacre at The Little Big Horn and later participated in the Buffalo Bill Wild West shows. These shows, recreated after the closing of the original frontier, usually portrayed Native Americans as savages. Yet, Sitting Bull was so stunned by the poverty he saw in America's big cities that he often gave the money he earned in these shows to the poor and homeless he met on the city streets.[7]

The irony was immediately apparent. Will Rogers was part of a Native American heritage that had often been treated shabbily and even violently by the American government during the westward movement. Yet, he became a spokesperson for a country that had taken over his ancestors' lands and driven out his own people. I realized his story was not just a story that acknowledged the remarkable achievements of a favorite son. It was a guide to a nation's future if its diverse population hoped to live in peace as people from different, even formerly antagonistic backgrounds.

Will Rogers united the many disparate elements of his Native and white American ancestries. It took a few more decades after his death to make us more aware of this richer, more complex picture of the earliest Americans. But it was a start. Yet, it was more than that. In his humor, he elevated the plight of the common man and woman who, throughout history, had often been slighted even as they did the work the world needed to be done for everyone.

In the months that followed, I plunged deeper into writing Will's story from my own personal perspective as someone who had, through accident and coincidence, found the "place" that author Eudora Welty felt was the most important element in writing fiction or nonfiction. That "place" was Will's ranch in Pacific Palisades I had visited many times in the last decade of the twentieth century. I realized we would be honoring Will Rogers again on August 15, 2035. He's been gone for almost a hundred years. What could he possibly teach us that we don't already know, or think we know in a vastly different nation than the one he experienced?

As I pondered that question, I asked myself, "If I had the power to bring back ten or twelve people from human history to meet with me and have a roundtable discussion of just how far the human race has advanced since we first set foot on this planet, who would I invite to that discussion?"

Part of that question was easily answered. I would invite very few, if any, political leaders from the past to that roundtable, although they are the ones who take up most of the space in history books. Some political leaders have tried diligently to make life on this planet more bearable for everyone. Too many of them throughout the world have chosen to acquire as much wealth as possible in one lifetime, and then to have that gold and silver buried with them rather than share it.

No, political leaders have already received too much attention in our history books. I realize I am revealing my own bias, but I would look to the arts and literature to share their opinions on how far we have advanced or regressed from century to century. Michelangelo, Da Vinci, Shakespeare, Tolstoy, Melville, Twain, Wharton, the Bronte sisters, and a host of other literary and artistic figures would have to be considered. I would also want Will Rogers to be a part of that group to share his common sense and homespun wisdom.

Will Rogers may not have been in their league as a writer or artist. He never claimed that he was. But he left behind a legacy of human decency and witty, humorous insights that force us to stop and think about who we are, and what we have to show for our own short stay on this small planet.

Maybe there would be someone better suited to join the illustrious group of world-renowned artists and literary figures whose genius still stun us with their remarkable insights into humanity's many strengths and weaknesses. But celebrity status settled lightly on Will Rogers's shoulders. Scandal never erased his accomplishments or tarnished his legacy. Wealth never corrupted him and created a self-perpetuating greed and unquenchable need for more wealth.

He was a fundamentally decent man, one who left the world better than he found it. He wasn't the greatest at anything, except maybe his rope tricks—but he was darn good at many things. No one before or since has spoken quite so effectively to the needs of the common folk who do the necessary hard labor to keep every society functioning.

Will Rogers's philosophy was relatively simple. Be kind to people. Never take yourself too seriously. Teach others to laugh. He urged us to remember that we are all ultimately one race of people struggling to survive on a planet that is not always conducive to our survival.

As I continued to work on this book, I would occasionally glance at the television screen in the living room and see the ruins that had been left behind after the wildfires passed through Pacific Palisades. Somewhere in all that rubble, I knew firefighters would eventually find some of the burned and charred mementos from Will's home. They would also remove the debris from the polo field where he would enjoy his friends and, perhaps, recreate his earlier life while riding on horseback across the Oklahoma prairie.

The Pacific Palisades wildfire, as cruel and horrible as it was, also saw great acts of kindness and humanitarian empathy. There was some looting, and the cause of the fire was suspicious. Still, there were many recorded acts of people working together to save lives and limit the destruction. Some who had vehicles pulled their neighbors who were stranded, including dogs and other pets, into their cars only moments before the wildfire engulfed their homes. Others stayed until the very last minute, spraying their neighbors' houses with water from garden hoses in the hope that it might save those structures. Still others rescued their neighbors who were trapped or unable to start their cars. These acts of empathy and compassion were reminders of Will's life. He had often traveled across America and to distant parts of the world to help those who had suffered similar losses.

In its fierce, unrelenting, destructive surge across Pacific Palisades and other sections of Los Angeles, the wildfire was an ironic reminder that we are all dependent on one another. The wildfire that caused so much destruction often revealed the better side of human nature that strives to improve the common good. It reminded us that we are all human, and our very survival often depends on our ability to work together.

It spite of these valiant efforts, the devastation was almost complete. The nation would have to find some way to put it all back together again. So much of Will Rogers's dream of a better, more caring nation seemed to have been deeply compromised or lost altogether. Those of us who are older and remember a nation that was less divided still feel his presence, his message of hope.

The inevitable comparisons between Will Rogers and Mark Twain are helpful. Twain was born in Missouri in the very middle of the continent. This enabled him later in his life to avoid a strictly "regionalist" label as a writer and author. He could claim, and rightfully so, that his literary voice was the "voice" for the entire nation, even a nation divided over the issue of slavery.

Will Rogers was also born in the middle of the continent. His Oklahoma heritage made him a Northerner, Southerner, Easterner and Westerner—all packaged in one individual. Like Twain, he was also a voice for the entire nation. He blended his white American heritage with his Native American ancestry. He spoke of those connections in one voice. It was not a voice filled with anger or contempt for one side of his heritage or the other. It was a voice that encouraged all Americans to live together in peace and with respect for our differences.

Will Rogers's entire life's journey was devoted to bringing us together. He did not dwell on the negatives. He dwelt on the ability of Americans, in spite of their differences, to forge a common destiny. It little matters whether it was the man or the myth that encouraged us to be a more peaceful and caring people. It little matters whether so much of that legacy is buried in the charred remains of his home in Pacific Palisades.

His life's legacy is that he worked to bridge differences through humor, not make them even more divisive. He emphasized our common humanity, not the differences in the way we speak or the color of our skin. He rose above all of that. He encouraged us—all of us—to work together for a more hopeful and peaceful future.

Without preaching, but instead by promoting laughter, Will Rogers transcended his time and place in history. He did not do this by excoriating those in power. He did it by reminding them they were not infinitely powerful. They too were limited, as we all are, by our imperfections.

Yes, I would like to meet Will someday and have a talk with him in the library of his ranch home in Pacific Palisades if it is restored. I feel like I had that talk with him several times thirty years ago, when I sat in his chair and felt his presence. Just him and me, and those wonderful stories he left behind.

I think I know now why he loved to twirl that rope of his in ever-widening circles. He wanted to include everyone in its magical power.

There are currently no plans to rebuild the ranch and museum at Pacific Palisades. Perhaps it doesn't matter. If he were here today, standing next to the charred, darkened ashes of his home after the wildfires destroyed it, I think he would still have urged us to be hopeful of a better future.

His gift of laughter was a gift of hope.

---

1. "Will Rogers and Wiley Post Killed in Airplane Tragedy," *The Longview Daily News* (August 16, 1935).
2. "Will Rogers and Wiley Post Are Killed in Airplane Crash," *The Evansville Press* (August 16, 1935).
3. "Will Rogers and Post Killed." *The Daily Ardmoreite* (August 16, 1935).
4. "From Cowboy to Film Idol, Rogers Life," *New York Daily News* (August 17, 1935).
5. "Cherokee Nation. Cherokee Roll." This is the form Will's father filled out to officially enroll his son in the Cherokee Nation.
6. Vincent Schilling, "Will Rogers was always a Cherokee," *Indian Country Today*, November 21, 2020.
7. "Who was sitting Bull?" Sitting Bull College. Sittingbull.edu/about/history/who-was-sitting-bull/

Wiley Post and Will Rogers pose by their airplane shortly before their deaths in Point Barrow, Alaska, on August 15, 1935. In the last years of his life, Will seemed to be searching for some new frontier to replace the one in Oklahoma where he had been born and raised. Leonhard Seppala, 1935. Wikimedia.org. Public Domain.

WESTERN UNION

FAIRBANKS, ALASKA AUG 15 1935

MISS MARY ROGERS.

SCOWHEGAN.MAINE.

GREAT TRIP WISH YOU ALL WERE ALONG, HOWS YOUR ACTING, YOU AND MAMA WIRE ME ALL THE NEWS TO NOME. GOING TO POINT BARROW TODAY FURTHEREST POINT OF LAND NORTH ON WHOLE AMERICAN CONTINENT.

LOTS OF LOVE, DONT WORRY.

DAD.

Will's telegram to his daughter telling her "DON'T WORRY" about him. Only hours later he died in the airplane crash. California State Parks, microfilm collection.

The plane crash site in Point Barrow, Alaska. Will and Wiley died only moments after the plane took off. *The Orion*, near Point Barrow, Alaska, 1935. The Gateway to Oklahoma History. Oklahoma Historical Society Photograph Collection.

Will's funeral at Forest Lawn Cemetery, Los Angeles, attracted mourners from everywhere. In other parts of the country, everything came to a halt as people paused to say goodbye to their Oklahoma cowboy. Courtesy of UCLA Library, Special Collections.

The shadow of an airplane flying near the crash site monuments at Point Barrow, Alaska, where Will and Wiley died. Naval Arctic Research Laboratory, 1973. Monuments at the Rogers-Post Site. Wikimedia.org. Public Domain.

The ruins of Will Rogers's ranch home in Pacific Palisades after the wildfire of January 7, 2025. The home Will had labored to transform into his childhood home in Oklahoma has been reduced to a burnt, charred pile of ashes and two stone-quarried chimneys. Copyright and courtesy of California State Parks.

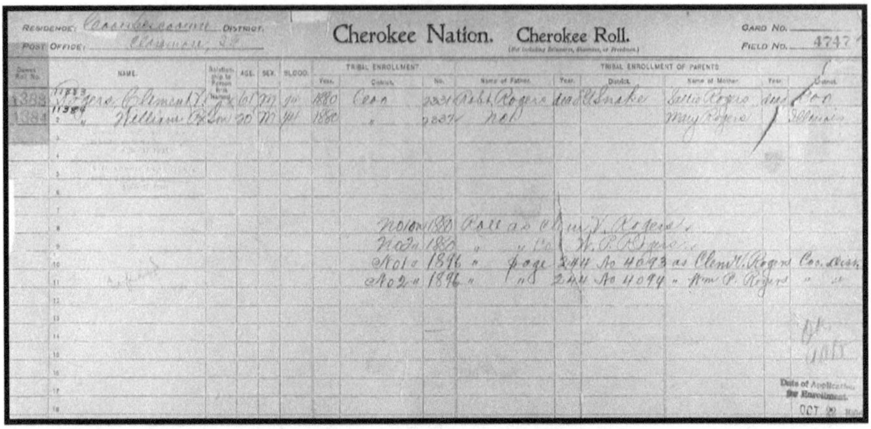

The Cherokee Nation Roll application filled out by Will's father, who also entered "William P., son," which added Will to the roll of the Cherokee Nation. Will was proud of his Cherokee heritage and never lost sight of his connections to his Native American roots. Dawes Enrollment Cards for Cherokee, Citizens by Blood, 1900. National Archives, Kansas City.

The statue of Will Rogers in the nation's capitol. After his death, Will's contributions to America were recognized by a grateful nation that voted to place his statue in a prominent place in the capitol. That statue can often be seen in the background when contemporary politicians are interviewed by the press. Will's good-natured, warmly smiling presence still hovers over our country like a father figure urging us to act wisely and with good humor as we move into the future. Harris & Ewing photographers, 1939. Will Rogers Statue, Capitol. Library of Congress.

# EPILOGUE

FOR TEN months after the wildfires swept through Pacific Palisades, the winding road leading up to the Will Rogers ranch was closed. A sign with the words "Road Closed" and several orange cones blocked the entranceway. The only thing one could see on top of the tree- and brush-covered hillside was a section of a white wooden fence. It appeared to be what was left of the longer fence that once enclosed the polo field.

In some ways, the sign seemed to be a fitting reminder that the era of Will Rogers was gone, closed forever.

Or was it?

Maybe the way he looked at himself as a humorist, storyteller, adventurer, humanitarian—the list is very long—was, like the ranch itself, waiting for a rebirth.

"Road Closed" sign with wilted flowers at the upper entrance to Will Rogers State Historic Park. Author's personal collection.

Then, on November 10, 2025, the California State Historic Parks, Palisades community, and park partners announced that the Will Rogers State Historic Park had been reopened for some activities. Trails and spaces were once again ready for the public to enjoy. The announcement added that although "the future of the ranch is still uncertain, the Rogers family is pleased to see the park open to the public—a place that has long been and will continue to serve as a living tribute to Will Rogers himself."

Now that the "Road Closed" sign has been removed, perhaps someday the buildings at the top of the hill can also be restored so we can revisit the ranch as Will designed it.

Will spoke to us in measured, whimsical tones, filled with wit and good humor. While the world during the last years of his life was moving toward the longest and most destructive war in history, he still retained his optimism that we were better than we often appeared to be.

Maybe someday we will hear his voice again and look to the future with renewed hope. Maybe we will again be a better nation because of his stories and faith in all of us.

# BIBLIOGRAPHY


Alworth, E. Paul. *Will Rogers*. New York: Twayne Publishers, 1974.

Aswell, James R. *Native American Humor*. New York: Harper & Brothers Publisher, 1947.

Bellamy, Glady's Carmen. *Mark Twain as a Literary Artist*. Norman: University of Oklahoma Press 1950.

Bercovitch, Sacvan. *The American Puritan Imagination. Essays in Revaluation*. London: Cambridge University Press, 1974.

Blair, Walter, and Hamlin Hill. *America's Humor From Poor Richard to Doonesbury*. New York: Oxford University Press, 1978.

Blair, Walter. *Native American Humor*. San Francisco: Chandler Publishing Company, 1937.

Boorstin, Daniel J. *The Americans, The Democratic Experience*. New York: Vintage Books, 1974.

Bradford, William. "*From History of Plymouth Plantation* (1620–1647)," *The Literature of America: Colonial Period*. ed. Larzer Ziff. New York: McGraw-Hill Book Company, 1970.

Bradley, Scully. *Our Native Humor: Critical Essays on American humor*. ed. William Bradford

Clark and W. Craig Turner. Boston: G. K. Hall & Co., 1984.

Brashear, Minnie M. *Mark Twain, Son of Missouri*. Chapel Hill: University of North Carolina Press, 1934.

*Chronicle of America*. ed. Clifton Daniel. New York: Prentice Hall Trade, 1990.

Clark, William Bedford, and W. Craig Turner. *Critical Essays on American Humor*. Boston: G. K. Hall & Co., 1984.

Clemens, Sam. See "Mark Twain."

Cobblestone Magazine. ed. Carolyn P. Yoder. Vol. 5, number 5, May, 1984.

Covici, Pascal J. "Mark Twain and the Old Southwest," *Critical Essays on American Humor*, eds. William Bedford Clark and W. Craig Turner. Boston: G. K. Hall & Co., 1984.

Cox, James M. *Mark Twain, The Fate of Humor*. Princeton: Princeton University Press, 1966.

Cox, S. S. "From *Why We Laugh* (1875–1876)," *Critical Essays on American Humor*, eds. William Bedford Clark and W. Craig Turner. Boston: G. K. Hall & Co. 1984.

Crane, Stephen. *The Great Short Works of Stephen Crane.* Harper and Row, 1965.
Croy, Homer. *Our Will Rogers*. Boston: Little, Brown and Company, 1953.
Day, Donald. "Letting Will Rogers Lasso Himself," *The Autobiography of Will Rogers.* Boston: Houghton Mifflin Company, 1949.
Day, Donald. *Will Rogers, A Biography*. New York: David McKay Company, Inc. 1962.
DeVoto, Bernard. *Mark Twain's America.* New York, 1932.
Durham, Phillip, and Everett L. Jones. "Introduction," *The Western Story, Fact, Fiction and Myth*. New York: Harcourt Brace Javanovich, Inc., 1975.
Earl, Edward A. "*Memorandum to Mr. Jack Welch.*" 16 February 1970.
Fitzgerald, F. Scott. *The Great Gatsby*. New York: Charles Scribner's Sons, 1925.
Franklin, Benjamin. *Autobiography*. New York: Holt, Rinehart and Winston, 1964.
———. "Silence DoGood No. 4," *Anthology of American Literature, Vol. I*: Colonial Through Romantic, ed. George McMichael. Macmillan Publishing Co., Inc. New York.
Gates, David. "*Same Twain, Different Time,*" Newsweek. 20 July 92.
Harris, Joel Chandler. *From "Humor in America"* (1909)], *Critical Essays on AmericanHumor*, eds. William Bedford Clark and W. Craig Turner. Boston: G. K. Hall & Co., 1984.
———. *The World's Wit and Humor: American*. New York: 1906. I.
Haweis, Reverend H. R. "From American Humorists (1882)," *Critical Essays on AmericanHumor*, eds. William Bedford Clark and W. Craig Turner. Boston: G. K. Hall & Co. 1984.
Hawthorne, Nathaniel. "The Custom House." *The Scarlet Letter.* New York: New American Library, 1959.
———. *The Scarlet Letter*. New York: New American Library, 1959.
Hofstadter, Richard. *Anti-intellectualism in American Life*. New York: Alfred A. Knopf, 1970.
Inge, M. Thomas. *The Frontier Humorists*. Hamden, Connecticut: Archon Books, 1975.
Isaacson, Walter. *Benjamin Franklin An American Life*. New York: Simon and Schuster Paperbacks. 2003.
Jacobs, Lewis. *The Rise of the American Film*. New York: Teachers College Press, 1968.
Kaplan, Justin. *Mr. Clemens and Mark Twain*. New York: Simon and Schuster, 1966.
Keough, William. *Punchlines, The Violence of American Humor*. New York: Paragon House, 1990.
Ketchum, Richard M. *Will Rogers, His Life and Times*. New York: American Heritage Publishing company, 1973.
Kirk, John G. *America Now*. New York: Atheneum, 1968.
Lamb, David. "Wild West Life: Sweet It Wasn't," *Los Angeles Times* 27 April 1988: A1.
Lang, Andrew. "From 'American Humor' (1889)," *Critical Essays on American Humor*, eds. William Bedford Clark and W. Craig Turner. Boston: G. K. Hall & Co., 1984.
Malone, Michael P. *Historians and the American West.* Lincoln: University of Nebraska Press, 1983.
Marx, Leo. *The Machine in the Garden.* New York: Oxford University Press, 1967.
McDermott, John Francis. ed. *The Frontier Re-examined.* Chicago: University Of Illinois Press, 1967.

McMichael, George. *Anthology of American Literature*: I. Colonial Through Romantic: New York: Macmillan Publishing Co. Inc., 1974.

Meine, Franklin J. "Tall Tales of the Southwest," *Critical Essays on American Humor*, eds. William Bedford Clark and W. Craig Turner. Boston: G. K. Hall & Co., 1984.

Miller, Perry. *Errand Into the Wilderness*. New York: Harper and Row, 1964.

Morton, Thomas. "From New England Canaan (1632)," *The Literature of America: Colonial Period*, ed. Larzer Ziff. New York: McGraw-Hill Book Company, 1970.

Murphy, Frances. Major American Poets. Lexington, Massachusetts: D. C. Heath and Company, 1970.

O'Brien, P. J. *Will Rogers Ambassador of Good Will Prince of Wit and Wisdom*. U.S.A. 1935.

Paine, Albert Bigelow. *Mark Twain, A Biography*. 3 vols. New York: Harper and Brothers Publishers, 1912.

Parrington, Vernon Louis. *Main Currents in American Thought*. New York: Harcourt, Brace & World, Inc., 1927. Vol. I.

Rickels, Milton. "The Grotesque Body of Southwestern Humor," *Critical Essays on American Humor*, eds. William Bedford Clark and W. Craig Turner. Boston: G. K. Hall & Co., 1984.

Rogers, Betty. *Will Rogers, His Wife's Story*. New York: The Bobbs-Merrill Company, 1941.

Rogers, Will. *A Will Rogers Treasury*. ed. Bryan M. Sterling and Frances N. Sterling. New York: Bonanza Books, 1982.

———. *Convention Articles of Will Rogers*. Stillwater: Oklahoma State University Press, 1976.

———. *Ether and Me*. New York: G. P. Putnam's Sons, 1935.

———. *"How To Be Funny" & other writings of Will Rogers*. ed. Steven K. Gragert. Stillwater: Oklahoma State University Press, 1983.

———. *The Autobiography of Will Rogers*. Boston: Houghton Mifflin Company, 1949.

———. *The Cowboy Philosopher on The Peace Conference*. Stillwater: Oklahoma State University Press, 1975.

———. *The Cowboy Philosopher on Prohibition*. Stillwater: Oklahoma State University Press, 1975.

———. *The Illiterate Digest*. New York: Albert & Charles Boni, 1924.

———. *There's Not a Bathing Suit in Russia*. Stillwater: Oklahoma State University Press, 1973.

———. *Will Rogers' Weekly Articles*. eds. James M. Smallwood and Steven K. Gragert. 6 vols. Stillwater, Oklahoma: Oklahoma State University Press, 1980.

Rollins, Peter C. *Will Rogers: A Bio-Bibliography*. Westport, Connecticut: Greenwood Press, 1984.

Rourke, Constance. *American Humor: A Study of the National Character*. New York: Doubleday & Company, 1931.

Sattelmeyer, Robert, and J. Donald Crowley. *One Hundred Years of Huckleberry Finn*. Columbia: University of Missouri Press, 1985.

Schilling, Vincent. "Will Rogers was always a Cherokee," *Indian Country Today*, November 21, 2020.

Schmitz, Neil. *Of Huck and Alice, Humorous Writing in American Literature*. Minneapolis: University of Minnesota Press, 1983.

Seitz, Don C. *Artemus Ward*. New York: Harper & Brothers, 1919.

Sewell, David R. *Mark Twain's Languages*. Berkeley: University of California Press, 1987.

Shakespeare, William. *Hamlet*. New York. Barnes and Noble Shakespeare, 2007.

Sloane, David E. *Mark Twain as a Literary Comedian*. Baton Rouge: Louisiana State University Press, 1979.

Smallwood, James M. and Steven K. Gragert. "Introduction," *Will Rogers' Weekly Articles*. Vol. 1. Stillwater: Oklahoma State University Press, 1908.

Sterling, Bryan M., and Frances N. Sterling. "Introduction," *A Will Rogers Treasury*. New York: Bonanza Books, 1982.

———. *Will Rogers in Hollywood*. New York: Crown Publishers Inc., 1984.

———. *Will Rogers World*. New York: M. Evans and Company, 1989.

Smith, Henry Nash. *Virgin Land, the American West as Symbol and Myth*. New York: Vintage Books, 1950.

Stout, Janice. *The Journey Narrative in American Literature*. Greenwood: Greenwood Press, 1983.

Sullivan, Ed. "Celebrities," *Will Rogers World*. By Bryan B. Sterling and Frances N. Sterling. New York: M. Evans and Company, 1989.

Tandy, Jennette. "An American Comic Character [From Crackerbox Philosophers (1925)]," *Critical Essays on American Humor*. eds. William Bedford Clark and W. Craig Turner. Boston: G. K. Hall & Co., 1984.

Trent, Spi. *My Cousin Will Rogers*. New York: G. P. Putnam Sons, 1938.

Trent, W. P. "A Retrospect of American Humor [1901]," *Critical Essays on American Humor*, eds. William Bedford Clark and W. Craig Turner. Boston: G. K. Hall & Co. 1984.

Turner, Frederick Jackson. *The Frontier in American History*. New York: Henry Holt and Company, 1921.

Twain, Mark. *The Autobiography of Mark Twain*. New York: Harper & Brothers, 1959.

———. How to Tell a Story," *The Norton Anthology of Literature*. New York: W. W. Norton and Company, 1989. Vol. 2.

———. *Innocents Abroad*. Hartford: The American Publishing Company, 1903.

———. *Roughing It*. Hartford: The American Publishing Company, 1903.

———. *Adventures of Huckleberry Finn*. New York: Barnes and Noble Classics, 2003.

———. *Adventures of Huckleberry Finn*. New York: The Bobbs-Merrill Company, Inc., 1967.

———. *The Complete Essays of Mark Twain*. Garden City, New York: Doubleday & Company, Inc., 1963.

Van Doren, Carl. *Benjamin Franklin*. New York: The Viking Press, 1938.

*Will Rogers Library*. Will Rogers State Historic Park. Santa Monica, California.

Will Rogers Memorial Museum Archives, Claremore, Oklahoma.

*World Book Encyclopedia*, Vol. 1. Chicago: Field Enterprises Educational Corporation, 1977.

Wright, Louis B. *The Cultural Life of the American Colonies, 1607–1763*. New York: Harper and Row, 1962.

Yagoda, Ben. *Will Rogers A Biography*. University of Oklahoma Press, 1993.

Ziff, Larzer. *The Literature of America: Colonial Period.* ed. Larzer Ziff. New York: McGraw-Hill Book Company, 1970.

# ABOUT THE AUTHOR

DENNIS M. CLAUSEN's Minnesota small-town background provided the inspiration for many of his literary works. He is also a professor of American literature and creative writing at the University of San Diego.

*Will Rogers Storyteller* is a nonfiction book Clausen started in the early 1990s when his wife Alexa was working as a historian on the "General Plan" for the Will Rogers State Park. He put it aside for many years and then started working on it again in January of 2025 after the Pacific Palisades wildfires decimated the park. Although the book is still framed by his earlier drafts and experiences on the park, he expanded on the original concept to make the book a study of "American humor from the beginnings to the Oklahoma Cowboy."

He recently completed a trilogy that included *The Accountant's Apprentice* (2018), *The Return Of The Fifth Horseman* (2022), and *Apocalypse In Our Time* (2024). All of the books received strong reviews. Chanticleer International Book Reviews selected the third novel in the trilogy as a "Best Book" selection and one of five "Silhouetted books" in the thriller genre.

Sunbury Press also published *The Search for Judd McCarthy* (2018), a novel *Publishers Weekly* described as "an expertly written thriller, a kind of Stephen King—Ross Macdonald hybrid (and in a class with either)." *The Sins of Rachel Sims* and *My Christmas Attic* were also published in 2018. NetGalley.com described *My Christmas Attic* as "a brilliant novel about a young dyslexic child who wants Christmas to last forever." Clausen has also written *Prairie Son* (1999), a widely acclaimed work of creative nonfiction about his father's struggles to survive in his adoptive home during the Great Depression.

Clausen's full biography and complete list of publications are available at www.dennisclausen.com.

www.ingramcontent.com/pod-product-compliance
Lightning Source LLC
LaVergne TN
LVHW090609110826
845146LV00001B/311

*9798888194256*